Editor

Sara Connolly

Cover Artist

Brenda DiAntonis

Managing Editor

Ina Massler Levin, M.A.

Creative Director

Karen J. Goldfluss, M.S. Ed.

Imaging

James Edward Grace

Publisher

Mary D. Smith, M.S. Ed.

Internet Literacy

Grades 6-8

Learn how to teach . . .

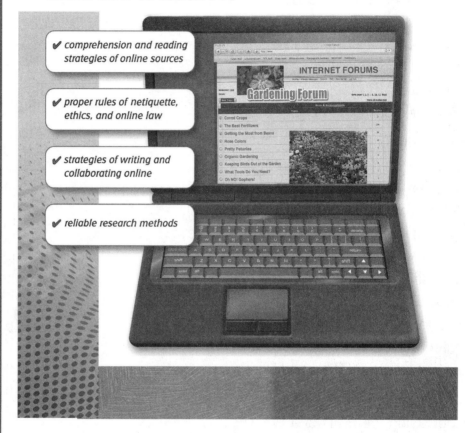

- ✔ comprehension and reading strategies of online sources
- ✔ proper rules of netiquette, ethics, and online law
- ✔ strategies of writing and collaborating online
- ✔ reliable research methods

Author

Heather Wolpert-Gawron

Teacher Created Resources, Inc.

6421 Industry Way
Westminster, CA 92683
www.teachercreated.com

ISBN: 978-1-4206-2768-8

© 2010 Teacher Created Resources, Inc.
Made in U.S.A.

Teacher Created Resources

Table of Contents

Table of Contents *(cont.)*

Foreword

Students are using the Internet daily. They use social networking sites, online malls, chat rooms, and browsers. But for the most part, they have learned these tools through a game of "telephone," from person to person, with no formal training in the Internet's specific literacy. Think of it as if all the books in the world were open to our students, but nobody was teaching them how to read, how to comprehend their information, and how to use it responsibly.

We as teachers are present for an evolution in education, including subjects and information that were not taught during our own school years, which now must be a part of our students' education. So educators must now don the hats of both teacher and student, playing catch-up in our own awareness. If we were to ignore the evolution that is occurring, that of online informational hunting and gathering, then we would not be doing our job of preparing students for their futures.

For an idea of why we are responsible for teaching Internet literacy, check out Matthew Needleman's "Mr. Winkle Wakes," a prolific short film dedicated to the importance of teaching with intelligent technology use in the schools:

http://www.needleworkspictures.com/ocr/blog/?p=289

As educators, it is also our job to continue integrating essential thinking skills when using these 21st Century tools. Just because Google™ finds information for a student, doesn't mean that we no longer teach how to doubt, research, and verify. And just because our students can use Facebook doesn't mean that they understand netiquette and collaboration.

How students read, analyze, disseminate, and evaluate all the information out there must be taught, and it is its own literacy. If we want students who are responsible online, we as educators must have a voice in their learning.

But Internet literacy is not just about website analysis. It goes a step further. It requires an understanding of three-dimensional reading and of comprehension in layers as a reader dives deeper and deeper, from link to link, seeking the information that they are seeking. And along the way, they are socializing, networking, collaborating, and gathering people to call for "informational lifelines."

Because of the interactive nature of the online world and the social two-way flow of communication, educators must make Internet literacy a vital part of the curriculum. It is more than just analysis; it's also about appropriate communication with the world at large. It cannot be acquired merely through participation or the fact that this generation was born into this technological world. It must be taught.

So it is education's duty to evolve, by teaching with technology and instructing students in how to read and disseminate the infinite supply of information out there. And it is also our responsibility to bridge the critical thinking gaps, laying the mortar of knowledge between the layers of technological tools.

An Argument for Why the Internet Is Its Own Genre

More and more studies are proving that reading on the Internet, that is, the skills that it takes to read and comprehend websites and webpages, requires its own lessons in literacy. We educators can no longer assume that a good "book reader" is also a "good Internet" reader any more than we can assume that a kid who can rattle off every character from *The Lord of the Rings* must also be able to read an instructional manual for setting up an iPhone.

Reading successfully online requires a hybrid of skills, and this, in turn, means that our schools must actively, and in a scaffolded manner, teach what those skills are in order for our students to navigate effectively.

There is a lot at stake if we do not teach these skills. It would be as if we were giving children cars and not giving them rules or the means to understand the street signs that keep them safe. They wouldn't know where to go, how to get there, or how to drive safely with others. So it is with online reading.

When we talk about the Internet as its own genre, we are talking about basic understanding of the following literacies:

1. basic reading skills
2. informational reading
3. visual literacy
4. skimming for information
5. multi-genre comprehension
6. three-dimensional reading (reading in layers)
7. critical thinking and decision making
8. social literacy (understanding peers through their writing)
9. computer-specific sentence structure (URLs, HTML, texting, etc...)

It is the very fact that reading online builds on every other genre and your knowledge of those genres that makes it its own genre category. In fact, author and educator Jim Burke stated on his English Companion Ning (a social network) that even Twitter™, an online social network that will be discussed in this book, "was officially validated as a genre...by being included in the latest AP Style Guide."

It is the fact that the Internet is a hybrid of all genres and then some that makes teaching it a particular challenge for educators.

After all, how can you teach Internet literacy effectively when your students are still learning what goes into a historic fiction book? That's where this book comes in. Each page is not only meant to be an activity, but also a reference. Even after the pages are completed, students should file them away in order to use them as future resources. This book is rich with the information that they will need in school and beyond.

What Is Internet Literacy?

Internet literacy includes the skills it takes to read, disseminate, and evaluate online sources. It is among the critical thinking skills that we as educators teach, empowering students as they venture online.

These are the questions of concern for Internet literacy:

1. How does a student evaluate fact vs. fiction, understanding authority and expertise vs. fraudulent sources?

2. What skills does a student need to know in order to evaluate a website and its level of trustworthiness?

3. How does a student combat the onslaught of the persuasive online advertising environment?

4. How does a student ethically decide what activities are appropriate to participate in online? How does he or she determine what is dangerous or illegal?

5. What does "intellectual property" mean to a student, and how does a student make an educated and ethical decision about his or her practices online?

6. How does a student communicate and collaborate with others in an online setting?

7. What are the rules of netiquette?

8. How does a student not only learn to read in a more online savvy fashion, but also to translate the learned 21st century skills into his or her writing?

All of these questions can only be answered through education. Students need to learn how to think critically. They need to trust that the computer might be fast, but it's not smart. Students need to be the smart ones.

Online, students are exposed to an infinite amount of information, and learning Internet literacy skills arms them with the ability to see their way through the forest of this information. Only through learning Internet literacy can students learn to make informed and safe decisions, while they produce work that assesses their knowledge of the skills that will prepare them for their future.

A Brief Note About Online Safety

Being safe online means using all of the skills that you learn in this book, and using them in the real world.

It means becoming a critical thinker who dives into the toolbox of knowledge to decide "Is this where I should go?" "Is this link safe to click on?" "Is this where I should be to get the information that I need?"

All these questions can be answered using the skills in this book. But a teacher using this book must also make sure that the students are aware of their transparency while online. In other words, everything you do online can be seen and read by others, so treat every piece of writing like it's a final draft that even the principal or a parent can read.

Don't believe this? Just do a Google vanity search by typing in a student's name and hitting Search. Even students who have never been online will find their names there. And many students will find comments or online contributions from years ago still present right there on the first search page of Google.

When online, students need to remember these five rules:

1. **Ask Questions.** Make sure you are near an adult so that you can ask questions and report anything suspicious.

2. **Keep private information to yourself.** Don't share your name, address, phone number, age, or school. Never send your picture to someone online.

   Keep your passwords private. And when you create a password, make sure it isn't obvious. Combine capitals and lowercase letters and numbers.

   Keep other people's information private as well. That includes your parents' workplaces, credit card numbers, addresses, or emails.

3. **Don't be tempted.** Don't enter contests or clubs without adult permission.

4. **Listen to your instincts.** If someone asks to meet you somewhere, to talk on the phone, or asks for your picture, tell an adult immediately.

5. **Follow the laws.** Never send mail that could hurt someone or make him or her feel threatened. Never copy commercial files without permission. Never use other people's passwords.

Remember, it's like roaming through the stacks in a library. Don't talk to strangers, and make sure you're in the aisle that you're supposed to be in. This book is meant to give students skills to make those decisions even when we're not around to help them.

It isn't scary. It's empowering.

Internet Safety Top Five Handout

Being online is like being in a really large neighborhood. You know some people better then others on your block, but you all follow rules to keep your neighborhood safe and enjoyable for everyone.

Keep this list posted or handy for reminders about the top five rules to keep you safe online.

While there are other things to remember online, if you only follow these five rules of safety, your online travels will be safer, more dependable, and more reliable.

1. **Ask Questions:** Make sure you are near an adult so that you can ask questions and report anything suspicious.

2. **Keep private information to yourself:** Don't share your name, address, phone number, age, or school. Never send your picture to someone online.

    Keep your passwords private. And when you create a password, make sure it isn't obvious. Combine uppercase and lowercase letters and numbers.

    Keep other people's information private as well. That includes your parents' workplaces, credit card numbers, addresses, or emails.

3. **Don't be tempted:** Don't enter contests or clubs without adult permission.

4. **Listen to your instincts:** If someone asks to meet you somewhere, to talk on the phone, or asks for your picture, tell an adult immediately.

5. **Follow the laws:** Never send mail that could hurt someone or make them feel threatened. Never copy commercial files without permission. Never use other people's passwords.

How to Use This Book

Reading a website has become its own genre of informational text, and as such, needs to be taught with very specific skills in mind. This book is meant to help prioritize some of the literacy lessons that one might teach to students in the 21st Century Classroom.

When we talk about differentiation, we have to include all forms of teaching, from traditional pencil and paper, to the use of technology. For that reason, this book includes both online and offline opportunities to teach Internet literacy, as indicated by the label in the upper right-hand corner of certain pages. By giving both options, this book addresses equity, bridging the gap between those students who have computers at home and those who do not.

There is also a metacognitive element to this book that allows for students to reflect on the "whys" behind their decisions. This book also supports the theory that "those who are teaching are learning" in that it includes many activities that ask students to design, create, rate, and evaluate.

It begins with an overview of basic pre-teaching necessities and quickly launches into the skills that students must have in order to participate online responsibly, both as readers and collaborators.

Before we begin, however, it is important for students and teachers to know the concept of transparency. *Transparency* is the word we use when we talk about the lack of privacy that each user has when going online. For instance, emails are forever. Comments on blogs remain forever. Any personal information, photos, or stories can be seen by anyone who really wants to see them, even if you use a password. So talk to your students about their lack of privacy online. Talk about only posting what you would feel comfortable sharing in person. Talk about only posting what you would be okay seeing, say, 10 years down the line. Talk about what can and can't be shared online. This book is not meant to frighten but to enlighten, educating students about their online footprint so that they may be more savvy online citizens.

The next heads-up is that the Internet changes. It is ever growing and morphing. At the time of its printing, this book provided accurate websites for each activity, but it's always a good idea with any Internet activity to preview a given website prior to teaching about it. This is merely a precaution.

Each page dives deeper into the nitty-gritty of Internet use, like how to search skillfully, how to communicate non-offensively, and how to participate with responsibility. There are assessments, both pre- and post-, in many differentiated formats. Use those that most suit your style and your lesson.

We hope that this book becomes a valuable resource in both your own education of Internet literacy and in your students' online awareness and comprehension.

Standards

The lessons and activities in this book meet the following standards and benchmarks, which are used with permission from McREL.

Copyright 2009 McREL. Mid-continent Research for Education and Learning
4601 DTC Boulevard, Suite 500, Denver, CO 80237
Telephone: 303-337-0990 Website: **www.mcrel.org/standards-benchmarks**

Technology Standards

Standard 2. Knows the characteristics and uses of computer software programs
5. Uses Boolean searches to execute complex searches on a database
6. Designs and creates webpages and simple websites

Standard 3. Understands the relationships among science, technology, society and the individual
1. Knows that scientific inquiry and technological design have similarities and differences
2. Knows that science cannot answer all questions and technology cannot solve all human problems or meet all human needs
3. Knows ways in which technology has influenced the course of history
5. Knows ways in which technology and society influence one another
7. Knows examples of copyright violations and computer fraud (e.g., computer hacking, computer piracy, intentional virus setting, invasion of privacy) and possible penalties (e.g., large fines, jail sentences)
8. Knows etiquette rules when using the Internet

Standard 4. Understands the nature of technological design
1. Knows that the design process is a slow, methodical process of test and refinement
2. Knows that the design process relies on different strategies: creative brainstorming to establish many design solutions, evaluating the feasibility of various solutions in order to choose a design, and troubleshooting the selected design
3. Identifies appropriate problems which can be solved using technology

Language Arts Standards

Standard 1. Uses the general skills and strategies of the writing process
4. Evaluates own and others' writing
5. Uses content, style, and structure (e.g., formal or informal language, genre, organization) appropriate for specific audiences (e.g., public, private) and purposes (e.g., to entertain, to influence, to inform)
12. Writes in response to literature

Standard 4. Gathers and uses information for research purposes
5. Organizes information and ideas from multiple sources for a research topic
7. Uses appropriate methods to cite and document reference sources (e.g., footnotes, bibliography)

Standard 5. Uses the general skills and strategies of the reading process
2. Uses word origins and derivations to understand word meaning
4. Uses specific strategies to clear up confusing parts of a text
5. Understands specific devices an author uses to accomplish his or her purpose

Standard 7. Uses reading skills and strategies to understand and interpret a variety of informational texts
3. Summarizes and paraphrases information in texts
4. Uses new information to adjust and extend personal knowledge base
5. Draws conclusions and makes inferences based on explicit and implicit information in texts
6. Differentiates between fact and opinion in informational texts

Standard 9. Uses viewing skills and strategies to understand and interpret visual media
1. Understands a variety of messages conveyed by visual media
2. Uses a variety of criteria to evaluate and form viewpoints of visual media
5. Understands how language choice is used to enhance visual media
6. Understands how symbols, images, sound, and other conventions are used in visual media

Sample Publishing Form

Dear Parent/Guardian,

This year your student will be given opportunities to contribute to our classroom's online projects. By signing this permission form, you are allowing the teacher to publish your student's material online or in other reading formats as model examples of curriculum that have been developed for the classes. Throughout the year he or she may be asked to contribute essays, vocal performances, and other materials for podcasting and/or publication.

Podcasting is the creation of online audio and/or visual files that an audience can subscribe to, much like a magazine subscription. Blogs are online journals that other students can comment on in order to help a student improve his or her writing and questioning. Wikis are collaborative documents that allow students to create, revise, and edit work together from their own homes or workstations.

It's an exciting leap for our school to offer these opportunities to students. Thank you for allowing them to be a part of this Internet literacy learning experience.

Student Agreement:

I, _____, give my instructor permission to submit my work and/or performance for publication.

Parent/Guardian Agreement:

I am the parent or legal guardian of the above-named minor and hereby approve the use of the minor's work and/or performance for possible publication purposes.

_____   _____
      Signature   *Date*

_____
      Print Name

Internet Savvy Pre-Assessment

So you spend time online and you surf the web daily. But just how Internet savvy are you really? Know what an RSS feed is? How about a Hyperlink? Well, maybe some of these topics are familiar to you and some of them aren't; but before we launch into some serious Internet literacy, you need to rate your knowledge of some of the topics that this book will be discussing.

Read the following topics and rate your understanding. Be honest. This isn't a test and nobody's judging your answers.

Topics	4 (I could teach this subject, that's how much I understand it.)	3 (I get it, and I understand its purpose.)	2 (I get the gist of these things, but I still need a brush up on occasion.)	1 (What the heck is this?)
Netiquette				
Advanced Google Searches				
Twitter				
Identifying False Websites				
Evaluating a Good Website				
Online Collaboration				
Reading a Webpage				

So here we go. You might think you know how to read and comprehend online, but until it's taught to you, you're only dog-paddling instead of doing the freestyle.

Have fun, and surf safely!

Internet Terminology

The Internet has its own language, its own vocabulary. So, to make sure we are all talking about the same things, here is a list of words that will help you as we continue through this book.

Go down the list and rate your knowledge of all the words first. Then, you have two choices of places to go in order to find the definitions:

1. Go to the Google homepage at **www.google.com**. Type "Define:_____."
   Fill in the blank with the word that you want defined.

2. Go to **www.dictionary.com** for the definitions and type in the word that you need defined.

Use this list as a resource as you continue studying Internet literacy.

Word	Know It	Rings a Bell	No Idea	Definition
URL				
Netiquette				
Blog				
Wiki				
Banner				
Textbox				
Phishing				
Homepage				
Hyperlink				
Search Engine				
Web Browser				
Comment				

Internet Terminology *(cont.)*

Word	Know It	Rings a Bell	No Idea	Definition
Moderate				
Password				
Post				
Reader				
RSS feeds				
Tag				
Keyword				
Menu Bar				
Transparency				
Character				
Bias				
Bookmark				
Website				
Webpage				
Forum				
Avatar				
Peer-to-Peer File Sharing				

What Constitutes a Reading Genre?

There are two types of reading categories: fiction and nonfiction. Those can be further broken down into different genres. Some have unique characteristics, and some share similarities; but in all, these genres include readings that have common forms, audience, format, or styles. Fill in the following genres with at least three characteristics that are shared by types of reading within that category. The first one has been done for you.

Mystery	Historical Fiction
Suspense Foreshadowing Setting	
Science Fiction	**Poetry**
Website	**Myths**
Fantasy	**Folk Tales**
Young Adult	**Biography**
Romance	**Autobiography**

Acceptable Use Policy: Literary Analysis

Below is an excerpt from the AUP published by cybercrime.gov. These rules also provide a good framework for your student's use of computers at home, at libraries, or anywhere. After reading this model, answer the questions that follow.

Model Acceptable Use Policy

The school's information technology resources, including email and Internet access, are provided for educational purposes. In order to be allowed continued access to the school's technological resources, students must:

1. <u>Respect and protect the privacy of others:</u> Use only assigned accounts. Users may not view, use, or copy passwords, data, or networks to which they are not authorized, nor may they distribute private information about others or themselves.

2. <u>Respect and protect the integrity, availability, and security of all electronic resources:</u> Students must follow all rules and report security risks or violations to a teacher or network administrator. They may not destroy or trash data or other resources that do not belong to them without clear permission of the owner.

3. <u>Respect and protect the intellectual property of others:</u> Students may not infringe copyrights. (No making illegal copies of music, games, or movies!) Do not plagiarize.

4. <u>Respect and practice the principles of community:</u> Communicate only in ways that are kind and respectful. Report threatening or discomforting materials to a teacher. Do not intentionally access, transmit, copy, or create material that violates the school's code of conduct (such as messages that are threatening, discriminatory, or meant to harass) or create material that is illegal (such as illegal copies of copyrighted works). Do not send spam, chain letters, or other mass unsolicited mailings.

Consequences for Violation. Violations of these rules may result in disciplinary action, including the loss of a student's privileges to use the school's information technology resources.

Supervision and Monitoring. School and network administrators and their authorized employees monitor the use of information technology resources at school. Administrators reserve the right to examine, use, and disclose any data found on the school's information networks in order to further the health, safety, discipline, or security of any student or other person, or to protect property. They may also use this information in disciplinary actions, and will furnish evidence of crime to law enforcement.

I acknowledge and understand my obligations:

_____   _____
            Student   *Date*

_____   _____
          Parent/Guardian   *Date*

Acceptable Use Policy:
Literary Analysis *(cont.)*

Answer the following questions using the AUP on the previous page.

1. True or False:

   A school's technical resources, such as email or Internet access, are for entertainment purposes. **T/F**

2. True or False:

   These rules are cautionary measures for school use only. These rules do not apply for use with home computers. **T/F**

3. A student tells her friend her login password so that her friend can copy a song that she's downloaded during her free time. According to the AUP, what rule is broken by her sharing this information?

   A. Rule #1

   B. Rule #2

   C. Rule #3

   D. Both A & C

4. Paraphrase the following quote in your own words:

   "Do not intentionally access, transmit, copy, or create material that is illegal (such as copyrighted works)."

   _____

   _____

   _____

   _____

5. In a one-sentence summary, state what the words "acceptable use policy" mean.

   _____

   _____

   _____

   _____

Acceptable Use Policy:
Literary Analysis *(cont.)*

6. How would you research information if you were no longer allowed to use the school's information technology resources?

   _____

   _____

   _____

7. Where can you go to get more information on Acceptable Use Policies?

   _____

8. Go back to the document on page 16 and underline the subheadings.

9. Go back and circle all of the verbs. Then create a list of the verbs on a separate sheet of paper. Write their definitions next to the word. This list will become a content language list that serves as a resource for you when creating your own acceptable use policy.

Student-Created Component: On a separate sheet of paper, write a draft of an acceptable use policy. You may use the content language list of verbs to help in your paraphrasing. Create your own title and text, using combinations of full sentences, subheadings, and bullet points. Make sure you leave a line at the bottom for a student to sign and date.

Developing a Super-Strong Password

Make up a typical password on the line provided: _____

Now, turn to a peer and play 20 questions in order to guess each other's password.

Did your fellow student figure out your password?

Developing a password is not meant to be an extension of your personality. It's meant to be an unhackable code word that only you (and your parents) know.

Good rules to follow are these:

1. Use eight characters or more.

2. Don't use a word in the dictionary because hackers use programs to easily bust these.

3. Change your password every six months or so.

4. Use numbers and letters in your password.

If you insist on creating something that's meaningful to you, use a password that is a full sentence in length and morphs the language into something less obvious. For instance, rather than saying "You go, Dodgers!" you can say, "uG0dojrz."

Write a new password on the line below that incorporates all of the rules above.

_____

Another way to go is to use an online password generator. Some possibilities are:

Secure Password Generator
http://www.pctools.com/guides/password/

Secure Random Password Generator
http://www.random-password.net/

Random Password Generate Online Service
http://www.findpassword.com/random-password-generate-online-service.php

Creating a Graphic Organizer with readwritethink.org

As you all know, prewriting is important before any essay, and creating a graphic organizer is a great way to produce an easy prewrite that gets your ideas out fast.

There are many resources online that allow you to create graphic organizers like webs, outlines, and the one that we are going to produce right now: a Venn diagram.

A Venn diagram, as you know, is a visual way to compare two or three concepts. It allows you to immediately see the similarities and differences between those concepts.

Before we go online, let's create a brief Venn diagram analyzing the similarities and differences between how we used to communicate prior to the Internet and since the Internet came into being.

Then　　　　　　　　　　　　　　　**Now**

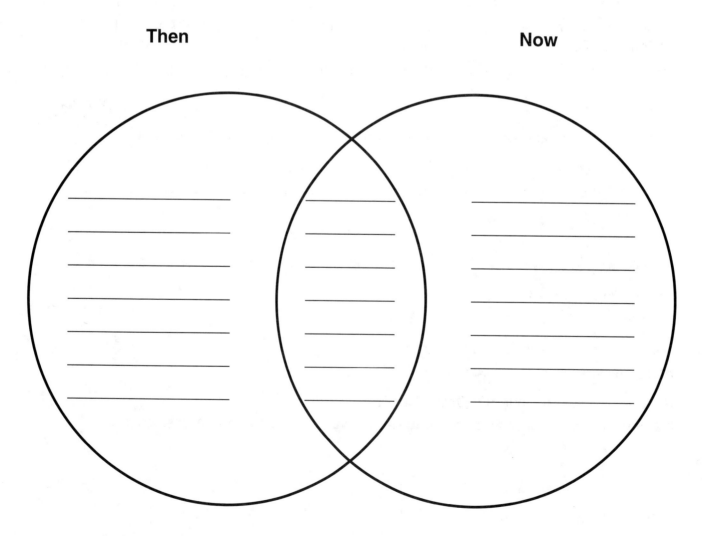

Creating a Graphic Organizer with readwritethink.org (cont.)

Now, let's learn how to use a great online resource to create a Venn diagram like the one you've just made.

Go to the URL **www.readwritethink.org**

Go to the left-hand menu and click on Student Materials.

Fill in the new URL here: _____

This is going to take you to a page that has a list of fantastic resources for your every graphic organizer need.

Scroll down the list and click on **Venn Diagram, 2 Circles**.

Fill in the new URL here: _____

(Notice that every page has its own [even slightly] unique address just as every house or business does.)

Click on the link that says **http://www.readwritethink.org/materials/venn/**

A little window opens up that asks you to label your Venn diagram and its circles. As you enter the information into the fields, you'll get new instructions on how to proceed. Follow the instructions from readwritethink to create your online Venn diagram.

When you are done, print it out, and turn it in to your teacher to show that you understand one way in which to use this great website.

Research

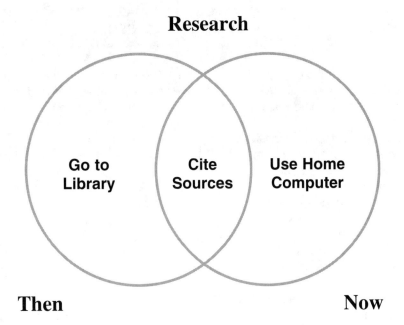

Go to Library   Cite Sources   Use Home Computer

Then   **Now**

Internet Literacy Vocabulary Crossword Puzzle

Directions: Unscramble the clues in the word bank. Then fill in the puzzle with the appropriate answers.

Word Bank

TETENIUQET	OBLG	PNSHHIGI	AGHOPEME	ANYPCNSERRAT
LRU	KIIW	RHPYILKNE	SSR	OEBSRRW

Across

2. A connection from one electronic document to another that can be triggered by the user, usually by clicking, causing another document to load in the browser
4. The attempt to fraudulently acquire sensitive information (e.g., passwords, account numbers, or financial information) by masquerading as a trustworthy person or business
7. A program or tool such as *Internet Explorer* or *Mozilla Firefox* that enables you to search and surf the World Wide Web and view Internet sites
8. A combination of two words: *Net* and *Etiquette*, refers to proper behaviors on a network
10. A contraction of the term "weblog," a type of website, usually maintained by an individual with regular entries of commentary

Down

1. The state of total visibility online, that is, anyone can read what was written, even years later
3. The opening page of a website
5. Really Simple Syndication, a newsfeed technology
6. A collaborative website which can be directly edited by anyone with access to it
9 Uniform Resource Locator: the address of a webpage

Student-Created Vocabulary Crossword

Creating your own crossword puzzle is an even better way to learn vocabulary. So let's learn how to use a great online resource to create your own crossword puzzle of Internet vocabulary words.

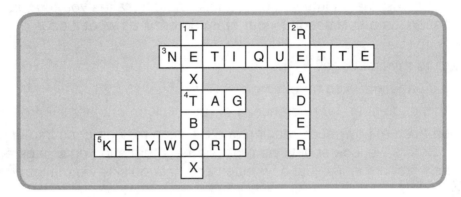

Go to the URL **www.readwritethink.org**

Go the left-hand menu and click on **Student Materials**.

Fill in the new URL here: _____

This is going to take you to a page that has a list of fantastic resources for your every graphic organizer and assessment need.

Scroll down the list and click on **Crossword Puzzles**.

Fill in the new URL here: _____

(Notice that every page has its own (even slightly) unique address just as every house or business does.)

Click on the link that says **http://www.readwritethink.org/materials/crossword/**

Follow the prompts to fill in your crossword puzzle. Begin by clicking on "Create your own." Then, fill in your name and the name of the puzzle. The name of your puzzle is "Internet Vocabulary."

Then begin to fill in a list of words that you want included in your crossword puzzle. Include at least 15 words in your puzzle. When finished, click on "Create Puzzle" and it will ask you to fill in your clues. The clues should be the definitions written in your own words.

After you've generated your own crossword creation, print it out, and turn it in to your teacher to show that you understand one way in which to use this great website.

The teacher might pass out other student crosswords to assess your knowledge of Internet vocabulary, so make sure you learn them all!

Internet Duration Log

One of the ways that reading online is so different from reading traditional texts is the quickness in which you need to make decisions. With each click to open or close a page, you are using critical-thinking strategies to determine if you are on the page that will help you the most. In other words, the minute you click a link, that link takes you to a page that gives your eyes information. In a split second, your brain determines what it sees and makes one of many decisions:

* Do I go back to my first page?
* Do I read this page and stop here?
* Do I leave this page open for reference later and click on another link from this page?

You would be surprised at how much reading and decision making goes into online comprehension. Before we look at how we process the information on a page and the skills it takes to do so, let's first recognize just how much and how quickly we make decisions.

Activity

Work with a partner. You'll need a timer or at least a view of the second hand of the classroom clock. One person will be the "thinker" and will control the mouse. The other will be the "recorder" who logs the URL to track the "thinker's" thinking patterns and times. Starting with the homepage of a search engine, log in the URLs of the pages your partner clicks on. Also, note how long your partner stays on each particular page before clicking away.

When you have found your answer, count the number of seconds and minutes it took to reach your goal. Just imagine how long it took to research before the Internet came along!

Here is an example. The guided question was "How many people on Earth use Twitter?"

Webpage	How Long?
www.google.com	10 sec
http://www.google.com/search?hl=en&client=safari&rls=en-us&q=how+many+people+use+twitter+on+earth%3F&btnG=Search&aq=f&oq=&aqi=	15 sec
http://onlinemediacultist.com/2008/03/31/how-many-people-use-twitter/	11 sec
http://twitterfacts.blogspot.com/2008/03/1-million-twitter-users.html	15 sec
http://www.google.com/search?hl=en&client=safari&rls=en-us&q=how+many+people+use+twitter+on+earth%3F&btnG=Search&aq=f&oq=&aqi=	25 sec
http://wiki.answers.com/Q/How_many_people_are_on_Twitter	12 sec
http://www.google.com/search?hl=en&client=safari&rls=en-us&q=how+many+people+are+using+twitter&aq=f&oq=&aqi=g	16 sec
http://www.dailyblogtips.com/how-many-users-does-twitter-have/	35 sec

Notice, we bopped back to Google and notated it here.

Total: 2:32

ONLINE

Internet Duration Log *(cont.)*

Choose one of the questions below based on your current subject and grade level:

1. How many plays and poems did Shakespeare write before his death?
2. Who first used a dodecahedron?
3. What were Ben Franklin's Top 10 Inventions?
4. Where did Gary Soto attend high school and college?

Webpage	How Long?

Total:

Extension Activity

Have the "thinker" now become the "recorder." The new recorder must now think of a question that ties into the subject matter of the class (maybe run it by your teacher for approval). Then time how long it takes the new "thinker" to come up with the answer.

Communication Then and Now

Long ago, people had to communicate through some very slow means. It's funny to think that The Pony Express used the word "express" like it was a fast method of getting from one point to another. It took days, sometimes weeks, to correspond. And now, when we drop a birthday invitation in the mail it only takes two days to arrive, yet we call it "snail mail" because it isn't instantaneous.

In 1860, Henry Wadsworth Longfellow wrote "The Midnight Ride of Paul Revere." It was a tribute to Revere's brave journey to warn the New England townsfolk of imminent British invasion.

You can use your textbook or go to the following website to read the poem in its entirety:

www.kidsandhistory.com/paulvm/h1_midride/ridepages_nosound/ridefset.html

According to Wikipedia, rhyme scheme is "the pattern of rhyming lines in a poem or song. It is usually referred to by using letters to indicate which lines rhyme. In other words, it is the pattern of end rhymes or lines. A rhyme scheme gives the scheme of the rhyme."

For example, in "The Midnight Ride of Paul Revere," the first stanza's rhyme scheme is as follows:

LISTEN, my children, and you shall hear	A
Of the midnight ride of Paul Revere,	A
On the eighteenth of April, in Seventy-Five:	B
Hardly a man is now alive	B
Who remembers that famous day and year.	A

Activity

Just as "The Midnight Ride of Paul Revere" was a poem describing how people communicated an important message long ago, you will create a poem about what it is like to communicate now.

On a separate sheet of paper, create a multiple-stanza poem that is about ways we communicate today. It could be about how a piece of information is transferred from one person to another. When you have completed your poem, pass it to a peer so that he or she can analyze its rhyme scheme.

Identifying the Parts of a Website

The minute you go online, you're bombarded by information in the form of text, graphics, ads, information, and entertainment. Being literate about a website means that you can identify the parts that make up a whole webpage and the purpose of each of those parts.

Look closely at the website at **edutopia.com** on the left in order to answer the questions on page 28.

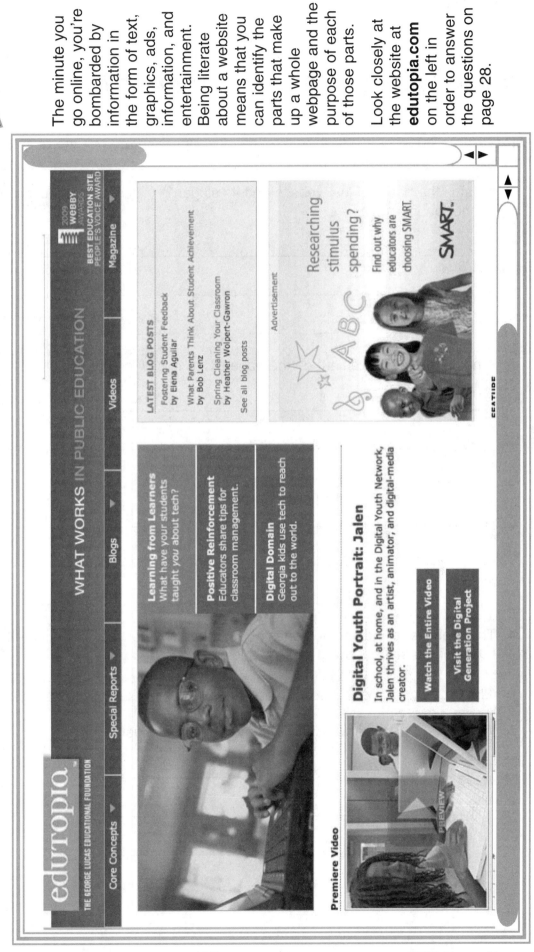

Identifying the Parts of a Website *(cont.)*

Directions: Study the website on the previous page and answer the questions to prove just how savvy a website reader you are.

1. What is the name of the website and its slogan? (These are generally located in the banner on the page.)

   _____

   _____

   _____

2. What is the advertisement on the page trying to sell to schools?

   _____

   _____

3. What are the three blog article titles?

   _____

   _____

   _____

4. This website tells different stories about student successes every week. What is the name of the student being profiled this week?

   _____

5. What award has this website won, and in what category?

   _____

   _____

   _____

28

Webbing a Website

Think about the concept of three-dimensional reading. Reading online is different than reading a traditional text because the reading is in layers. When webpage designers create a site, they first create a visual web to help them brainstorm where each piece of information is going to go and at what layer. We can trace a designer's thoughts by clicking through a completed site and creating a web for each page, or each layer, of the site.

The first page, the homepage, acts like a table of contents. It tells you where to click in order to get the information you need from the layers underneath. As you peel back a layer, the information gets more and more specific. The homepage is also a place for banners, ads, pictures, and menu bars.

Let's go to a school district and web its website.

Go to **www.sgusd.k12.ca.us**. This is the district website for San Gabriel Unified School District in Los Angeles, California.

As you can see, there is a banner on the top and various words in the menu bar that all have links. Let's web one of the tabs on the menu bar, the one marked "Our Schools."

Click on "Schools" in the Upper menu bar. Label each box beneath the homepage with one of the schools mentioned on the menu tab. The first one has been done for you.

Now click on the link for "Jefferson Middle School." You'll notice that their menu bar is on the side of the page. Menu bars can be on the top, bottom, left side, or right side on the page, so you have to know what you are looking for.

Webbing a Website (cont.)

Click on any three links under the heading "School Resources." Label the three pages in the three boxes below.

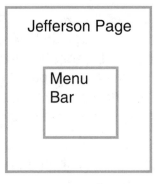

Jefferson Page

Menu Bar

Now pick one of the links that you chose to click on and follow its next layer of links by creating another set of boxes. Label these boxes as well.

These layers can go on forever…or they might end abruptly. It depends on their purpose and just how informative they are.

Extension Activity

Go to your district's website. If your school doesn't have a website, find a school district near you and go to a school webpage from their site.

On a separate sheet of paper, web the website. It might take a while, but you'll really appreciate the work and the effort that goes into creating a website. Each layer is a result of a decision that someone made to continue providing information for those who might need it.

Identifying the Parts of Your School's Website

A. Go to your school's website. (If your school doesn't have a website, go to a website for a nearby school or district.) Recreate it in the box provided. Try to get every box and every piece of text. You don't have to draw the images, but make sure you at least indicate the boxes where images appear. Make sure you include the **banner**, all **text boxes**, **image boxes**, and **menu bars**.

By ensuring that you can identify every element on a website, you can then make sure you understand the purpose of each element.

B. Based on the website, create five questions on a separate sheet of paper that ask a peer to analyze the website. Here are some sentence stems to help you develop your questions:

- What is the purpose of the…?
- Where is the slogan or mission statement…?
- What does the symbol…?
- What links are available to find…?

Identifying the Parts of Your School's Website *(cont.)*

C. Trade questions with a peer and see if their questions make you see the website and its elements in a different way. Answer the questions.

Final Project Notes

If you were designing a webpage, what elements from this website might you want to incorporate onto a homepage that represents you?

_____

_____

_____

_____

_____

_____

_____

What Are Your Eyes Doing?

Nonlinear Reading

One of the unique qualities of reading on the Internet, and one of the best arguments for the Internet as its own reading genre, is the physical way we read and comprehend pages. After all, your eyes don't move linearly. Rather than read left to right, from the top of the page to the bottom, like we do with a book or a magazine, our eyes jump all over the place on a webpage before settling on what we want to read.

Our eyes might start at the banner, then jump to the sidebar, and then leap to the headline of a post halfway down the page. When reading a website, your eyes dart from place to place, gaining meaning in an instant, determining if it's the page you need to be on.

Pretend that you have an assignment to go online and find the location of the Galapagos Islands.

Look at the website below. In the little circles besides each element of the website, write the number that represents where your eyes went first, second, third, etc. Then answer the questions that follow.

○ **The Galapagos Islands.com**

○ **Planning to visit?**

○ **The Geography of the Galapagos**

○ **Galapagos History Blog**

○ **Contact the Webmaster**

○ **GalTours**

What Are Your Eyes Doing? *(cont.)*

1. What part of the page did your eyes hit first? Why?

   _____

   _____

   _____

2. Which number is next to the link that might show you the answer to the question:

   Where are the Galapagos Islands? _____

3. Prediction: What do you think that link might connect you to?

   _____

   _____

4. Which number is next to the link that might tell you a little about the author of the website?

   _____

5. Which number is in the box that contains an advertisement?

   _____

6. The next time you are online, track how your eyes travel and think about why they followed the path that they did.

Final Project Notes

If you were designing a webpage, what elements from this website would you want to incorporate onto a homepage about you?

_____

_____

_____

_____

_____

What Are Your Eyes Doing? *(cont.)*

Three-Dimensional Reading

Not only do we read Internet pages in a non-linear way, but we also read them three-dimensionally. The links on a page allow us to create layers of information at our fingertips.

It's like when you read a book and put your fingers in the pages to hold them. Sometimes you run out of fingers, right? But on the Internet, you can hold as many pages as you want and interact with them in any order you want.

From page to page, you decide what link you want to pursue, click on that, and then (keeping the first page available to click back to) you click on link after link after link, creating a stack of pages in your hunt for the information you most want to read. As an online reader, you make quick decisions on what pages you want to keep open, which ones to close, which ones to click off of, which ones to bookmark, etc…

Let's look at this concept of three-dimensional reading.

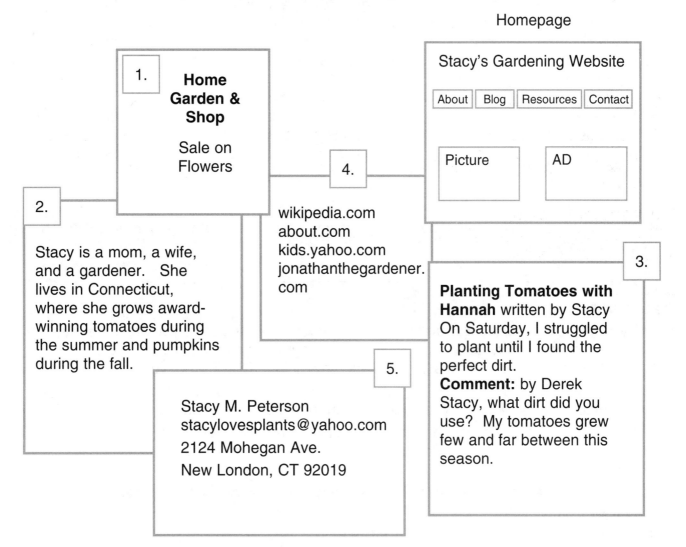

What Are Your Eyes Doing? *(cont.)*

Read the homepage and answer the following questions:

1. What are the four tabs in the menu bar?

   _____

   _____

2. A blog is a diary that people can comment on, ask questions about, and refer to. When you read someone's blog, you sometimes get advice without having to ask a question, because someone else may have asked it already. Which number page do you link to in order to read Stacy's blog?

   _____

3. Let's say you looked at the homepage and even though you meant to click on Stacy's information, you click on the advertisement instead. This link took you away from Stacy's page and onto a persuasive page. What page number did you link to?

   _____

4. If you want to email Stacy directly, which page do you link to?

   _____

5. Maybe you're looking to start your own garden and want to know other places that Stacy gets her information from. After all, there is tons of information out there and not one person can know it all. Sharing information with others is a part of the online neighborhood. What page do you click on to get her other suggested resources?

   _____

6. If you want to know a little about Stacy and what she does outside of gardening, which link would you click on?

   _____

Extension Activity

- Take a stack of index cards and write a paragraph about the story you are currently reading in your language arts class. In your paragraph, you should include the TAG (title, author, genre), a short summary, and an opinion. Don't forget your name!

- Underline the important words or phrases in the paragraph that a reader may want more information on. Make sure you underline your name as well. You are the author!

- Create a card for each word or phrase you underlined going further into information that is specific to just that word or phrase. The card based on your name should be the "About Me" card.

- Then underline words or phrases in those second tiers of cards that might also connect to their own explanation cards.

Voilà! Your very own offline version of a website.

What's the Purpose of the Website?

A website is a mix of genres and requires intense literacy skills from its reader to understand its purpose. It's important that when you read a website, you read it honestly, knowing where every element is coming from.

Look at the website on the left from **educationworld.com.** Analyze the purpose of its components by answering the questions on the following page.

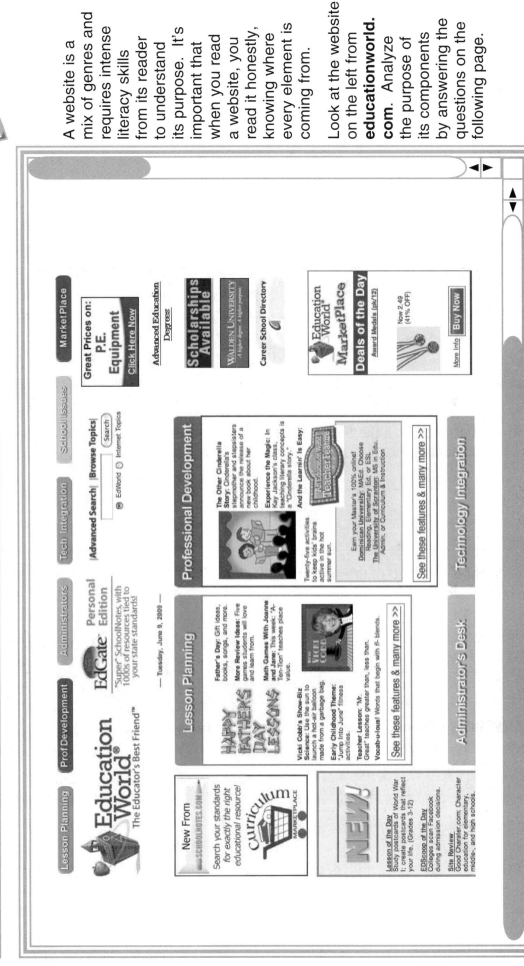

What's the Purpose of the Website? *(cont.)*

1. Members of what profession are reading this website?

   _____

   _____

   _____

2. Describe one advertisement on this page and towards whom it might be geared.

   _____

   _____

   _____

   _____

3. Of the six tabs at the top of the page, which one might you click on to read about educational news?

   _____

   _____

   _____

4. What is the logo of the website and why were its symbols chosen to represent it?

   _____

   _____

   _____

   _____

5. What is the purpose of the Education World Marketplace? _____

   _____

   _____

   _____

   _____

Phishing for You

According to wikipedia.com, **phishing** is "the criminally fraudulent process of attempting to acquire sensitive information such as usernames, passwords, and credit card details by masquerading as a trustworthy entity in an electronic communication."

In other words, phishing is a common way to dupe people into giving out personal information.

In May 2007, Indiana University researchers conducted an experiment. They sent out fake emails, phishing for students to take the bait just to see how Internet savvy their students were. Of the 600 students, 72% of them fell for the fake email! But that's not all.

According to a watchdog group, **www.antiphishing.org**, there are approximately 32,000 phishing attacks reported per month. And the victims are smart, educated people like you.

So what can you look for? Well, let's examine one to find out.

Below is an example of a phishing scam email:

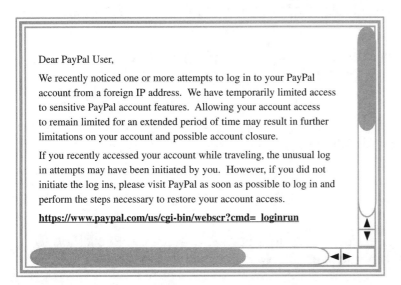

Dear PayPal User,

We recently noticed one or more attempts to log in to your PayPal account from a foreign IP address. We have temporarily limited access to sensitive PayPal account features. Allowing your account access to remain limited for an extended period of time may result in further limitations on your account and possible account closure.

If you recently accessed your account while traveling, the unusual log in attempts may have been initiated by you. However, if you did not initiate the log ins, please visit PayPal as soon as possible to log in and perform the steps necessary to restore your account access.

https://www.paypal.com/us/cgi-bin/webscr?cmd=_loginrun

Notice how vague this email is. In other words, there is nothing here that is specifically indicating that it is for you and only you. It isn't sent to a specific person. It doesn't mention a specific account. But if you were to click on the link at the bottom, it would ask you to enter those items to confirm your account.

Don't fall for it.

Ways to avoid being a victim of a phish attack are:

NEVER open an attachment or click on the link if you don't know the sender.

NEVER click on an email that is only identified by an IP address.

NEVER run an unknown program or plug-in. Don't download anything to your computer without completely trusting the source.

To see other examples of phishing emails, go to **http://antivirus.about.com/od/emailscams/ss/phishing.htm** and click each page of the article for true-life examples.

To report a fraudulent email or other phishing scam, email **complaint@ftc.gov.**

ONLINE

Skimming for Information

Many times when we are doing research online, we find ourselves skimming for information on a webpage to determine if we are on a website that we need. Great research starts with great resources. But after that, you must use your knowledge and critical-thinking skills to find the information that you are hunting.

There are online articles out there that are about any subject one could possibly imagine. One of the best websites to go to for up-to-date information on anything is **www.howstuffworks.com**. Let's go there now.

As you can see on the homepage, the latest articles are posted for you to click on. But at this time, find the search bar. It should be under the top advertising banner, next to the main titles.

Found it? Type "How does a space elevator work?" Now a page pops up with lots of text. Watch out! Some of that text is advertising, and shouldn't be used in your research.

Scroll down a little ways and you'll begin to see articles on space elevators and other related resources. There are multiple pages on the topic, so click on the one that says, "Introduction to How Space Elevators Will Work."

The article is a combination of text and images, and it is on multiple pages. Looking at the subheading listed underneath the title, how many sections are there in this article? _____

Click on the second section, the one entitled "Riding a Space Elevator to the Top." According to the **bold** type in the first paragraph, what are the three components of the elevator that can begin to be built using today's knowledge of technology?

_____

_____

_____

Under the subheading "Avoiding Space Debris," what three links are available to click on to find out more about the kinds of debris that might collide with the space elevator?

_____

_____

Extension Activity

Go back to the homepage and type the following science-related topic, "Barriers to Jet Pack Development." Answer the following questions about your topic:

1. What is the main idea of the article?

2. How many subheadings are there in the article?

3. Read the whole article and count the number of links that the article provides for further research. How many links does the article provide?

How to Read HTML

HTML is a computer language. For every click of the mouse, or press of a button, the computer translates your needs into HTML and that HTML produces what you want to see on the page. It's an invisible behind-the-scenes language that is always present, but rarely seen.

HTML stands for:

Hyper **T**ext **M**ark-up **L**anguage

Behind every page of text is the invisible HTML.

For example, let's look at the following two lines of text and the corresponding HTML:

Dear **Joe**,   Have you read *The Outsiders?*   Sincerely,   **Heather**

```
<br>
<br>
Dear <b>Joe</b>, <p>
<br>
Have you read <i>The Outsiders</i>?<p>
<br>
Sincerely, <p>
<b>Heather</b>
```

It's important to know a little about HTML because it comes up as you surf the web and also as you type documents on a computer. So just to touch on it a bit, let's write a little HTML ourselves:

KEY:

 = Break, as in every time you hit RETURN   <b> = Bold

<i> = Emphasis, as in adding italics to emphasize a word   <p> = paragraph

You put a slash at the start of the last bracket to indicate the end of the command.

On the following lines, write a one-sentence summary of a short story you are currently reading in your Language Arts class. Then, rewrite the sentence using HTML.

Normal Text:

_____

_____

HTML:

_____

_____

Extension Activity

Go to **www.google.com**. Notice that you can read it because it's in plain text. But if we pull back the layer on top of the website, you'll see the HTML. Go to your menu bar in your Browser and click on "View." Then click on "View Source." This should reveal the HTML that is used to create the webpage. It's a lot more complicated than just <b> and <i>, isn't it?

Reading an Amazon™ Page

Amazon.com (**www.amazon.com**) has become a huge way to shop for items online. It sells almost anything because it functions like the biggest mall you've ever been in.

Critical Thinking

Why do you think it's called "Amazon?" Write your response here:

_____

_____

But just like when you enter a mall for the first time, you can be overwhelmed if you don't know where to put your eyes. If you don't know how to get around a mall, sometimes you find yourself entering stores you didn't mean to go into, or even shopping for items you didn't need. Let's learn a little about how to find what we need in this mall so that we can get in and out without falling into any online shopping traps.

On the front page of Amazon, you'll notice a few elements that are similar to any store in any mall. Only here, there are pictures connected by links. Match what you see on Amazon to what you generally see in a store by filling in the blanks below:

A. Left-Hand Menu

B. Search Bar Above

C. Ads to click on

D. Books Frequently Bought Together

_____ Posters of products inside store

_____ Information Desk

_____ Signs at the end of aisles

_____ Mannequins with matching outfits

Answer the following questions to show your understanding of the Amazon homepage.

1. Let's say you wanted to recommend a soccer net to your coach, but you didn't know the brand that you wanted to buy. There are two ways to find soccer nets from the homepage. List the two ways to find it.

   • _____

   • _____

2. Let's say you ordered a new pair of pants. They arrived a few days later, but they were the wrong color. How could you find out how to return them? Look at the entire homepage (you may even need to scroll down) to find this answer. Describe the process of returning an item to Amazon on the lines below.

_____

_____

_____

_____

Reading an Amazon™ *Page* (cont.)

Teacher Note: Preview the Amazon page prior to teaching this lesson. Amazon moderates its own book reviews, but sometimes there's a delay. Just look ahead and make sure the reviews the students will be reading are appropriate for your grade level.

Now let's say that you are dying for a new book. But you really don't know what book to order. You don't have a title; you just know what kind of book you might be interested in.

Let's start by clicking on the left search tab towards the top of the page that defaults to (always starts with) Amazon.com. Click it and you'll see a list of categories appear.

Then click on **Books**. This tells you that Amazon is prepared to show you the bookstore part of its mall.

In the blank search bar, type in a literary genre such as "Science Fiction." Click **Go**. You'll be directed to the bookstore, and you'll notice immediately that the left-hand menu has changed.

Answer the following questions to help guide you to the part of the store that is right for you:

1. How many books are listed in the "last 30 days" New Releases link?

   _____

2. How many books are listed in the "Science Fiction & Fantasy" link?

   _____

3. How many books are listed in the "Children's Books" link?

   _____

4. How many books are listed in the "Teens" link?

   _____

5. How many books are listed in the "Comics & Graphic Novels" link?

   _____

Click on the **Teens** link at this time.

You'll now find that you are in the part of the bookstore that is both "Teens" and "Science Fiction & Fantasy."

Scroll down to Neil Gaiman's *The Graveyard Book*. If you don't see it right away, you can type in the title in the Search bar. This book is the 2009 Newbery Award winner. Click on the picture and you will be directed to the page about that particular book.

ONLINE

Reading an Amazon™ *Page* (cont.)

Scroll down this page to answer the following questions:

1. How much does this book cost?

_____

2. Who published this book?

_____

3. How many pages does this book have?

_____

4. What is the reading level, that is, for what ages is this book appropriate?

_____

The greatest thing about the Internet is that it allows people to get opinions from other people. By looking at this page, you can tell that others have read this book, and have also read other books that interested them. Name two other books that people who have read *The Graveyard Book* would recommend to others.

_____

_____

People who want to review a book are asked to rate the book by giving it stars. How many stars does *The Graveyard Book* average?

_____

Read through the reviews and you'll notice that the most informative have similar elements. They include powerful and persuasive word choice, and great evidence. Maybe they also mention certain elements they like from the narrative, like the plot, the characters, the setting, and the figurative language.

Final Project Notes

If you were designing a webpage, what elements from this website might you want to incorporate onto a homepage that represents you?

_____

_____

_____

_____

ONLINE

Using a Search Engine

There are multiple ways to hunt down information using a search engine. But first, you have to choose your search engine.

Google is a search engine that we use frequently, but there are others out there. Some even have different purposes and focus their research in unusual or more-specific directions.

Metasearches

According to Wikipedia, a metasearch engine is "a search tool that sends user requests to several other search engines and/or databases and aggregates the results into a single list or displays them according to their source."

There are many different metasearch engines that you can choose from. For instance, **www.dogpile.com**, and **www.search.com** are both metasearch engines.

Google can be used as a metasearch engine as well. Go to **www.google.com/dirhp**. You'll notice that you can now search by category. A very convenient way to search, wouldn't you say so?

Type "metasearch" in the field and click return. You'll be taken to a page that offers you tons of different search engines and their specialties.

Metasearch Activity

Go to **www.dogpile.com**. Type "History of the Titanic."

Now go to **www.search.com** and type the same search.

Did you see differences between the results from the first metasearch and the second? Are there websites that appear on both lists?

_____

_____

_____

_____

As you get to know different metasearch engines, you will find those you like using in your research more than others. Explore a bunch of them and expand your ability to research beyond the more common methods.

Using a Search Engine *(cont.)*

`ONLINE`

How to Search Effectively

The most common way to use a search engine, of course, is by using **keywords**. Keywords are the most important words or phrases you want a search engine to hunt for.

For instance, if your teacher asks you to research the History of Theater in the Renaissance, you could type in "History," "Theater," and "Renaissance."

Another way to search for your topic is through conducting a **Boolean search** (boo-li-an). A Boolean search allows you to seek out your topic in the form of a question. This permits an information hunter to phrase a question the way he or she might actually ask it of a person.

For instance, let's say you are doing a report on the adverse affects of tobacco. Type the keyword "Tobacco." How many results did you get? _____

Now type the question, "What are the adverse affects of tobacco?" How many results did you get now? _____

Web Browser Activity

Convert the following keywords into questions:

1. Keywords: book   Newbery   20th Century

   Question: _____

2. Keywords: blog   education   middle school

   Question: _____

3. Keywords: actor   Oscar   first

   Question: _____

Now convert the following questions into keywords:

1. Question: What is the route for the upcoming Tour de France?

   Keywords: _____ _____ _____

2. Question: On what continent has the Olympic Games most often been held?

   Keywords: _____ _____ _____

Extension Activity

Now write three keywords and have a peer convert them into questions. Then write a research question and have a peer convert it into two-to-three keywords.

How to Read a Google™ Search Page

Just because a result from what you typed appears on the first page of a Google search doesn't mean it's what you need to conduct your research. Let's say you are writing a science report on global warming. You go to Google to begin your hunt for straightforward information.

Let's look below at a screenshot of a Google search for the phrase "global warming" and see which links on the page might give you exactly what you need.

How to Read a Google™ Search Page *(cont.)* Offline

A "Sponsored Link" is a line you can click on to see an advertisement for a product. The words "Sponsored Link" are there to tell you that what you are about to click on will be **biased** and is not meant to inform, but to persuade. Don't fall for it!

1. How many sponsored links appear on the Google page after you type the words "global warming"?

   _____

Look at the URLs for each of the websites listed. Based on what you see here, which sites do you believe are most likely to give you the accurate, informative, unbiased research that you need?   Write their URLs in the lines provided.

2. _____

3. _____

4. Which site is created by the government and includes information for kids?   Write the URL on the line below.

   _____

5. How many book results are there? _____

What are other searches that Google advises to make your search more specific?

6. _____

7. _____

8. _____

9. _____

10. How many entries are there total on Google when searching with the keywords "global warming?"

   _____

Better Ways to Use Google™

Google allows for many different ways to search for information. Some methods are better than others, depending on what you want to research. Then again, sometimes you just fall in love with a certain method and that becomes the style you use most often. But knowing that there are other options out there increases your chance at finding information quickly and accurately with the fewest necessary search attempts. After all, if you get what you need right away, you've saved research time, right?

OK, let's say you want to write a research paper about using video games in education. Start by going to the Google homepage at **www.google.com**. Type "video games."

1. How many sites are available according to Google?

_____

Did you plan on searching through all of those options to find what you wanted? No, of course not.

So let's look at a number of the options Google gives you in order to conduct a quick and accurate search. After all, Google wants to save you time and effort, so take it up on its offer!

Let's look at the following:

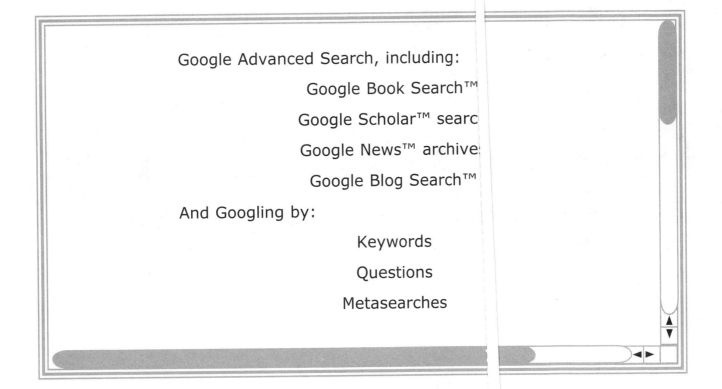

Google Advanced Search, including:

Google Book Search™

Google Scholar™ search

Google News™ archives

Google Blog Search™

And Googling by:

Keywords

Questions

Metasearches

Better Ways to Use Google™ *(cont.)*

Welcome to Google Advanced Search!

The greatest little-known tool is Google Advanced Search.

1. Go to the Google homepage and click on the link over there on the right of the field. When you click on that, you should be connected to a screen that looks like this:

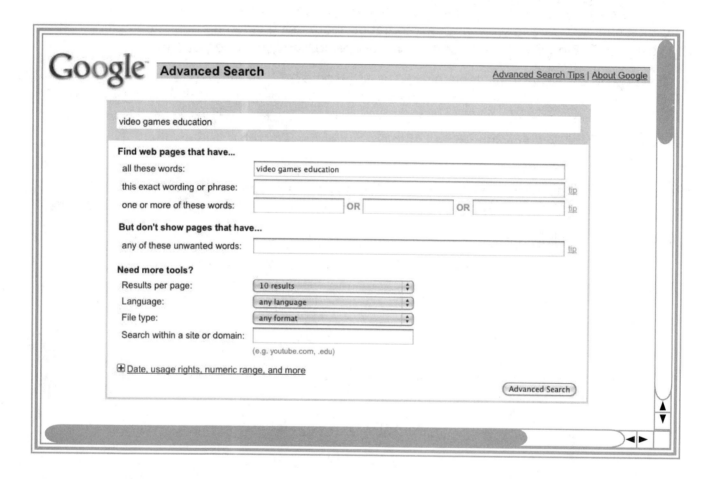

Be specific with your keywords. As you see in the screenshot above, in the field marked "all these words," you would type in the keywords "video games education."

ONLINE

Better Ways to Use Google™ *(cont.)*

2. Click return. How many results now appear?

_____

So what we've learned is that the more specific your keywords, the fewer the results. Great! But that number is still too many to search through, so we're going to use yet another tool. We're going to look in different Google "Libraries." Look down the page and check out the specific banks Google can draw its results from:

3. **Google Scholar:** Searches for results through, according to Google, "scholarly literature across many disciplines and sources, including theses, books, abstracts, and articles. Pretty good for up-to-date academic information." Click on Google Scholar and type in "video games in education."

How many results are available through Google Scholar?

_____

4. Now click on **Advanced Scholar Search** to the right of the field. In the Date field, type "2007"–"2009." For "Subject Areas," click on **Social Science, Arts, and Humanities**.

Now how many results are available?

_____

5. Now go back to the Advanced Search page and click on **Google Books**. Google Books has access to literally millions of libraries and publishers and their books worldwide. Now click on **Advanced Book Search** to the right of the field. In the "Search" field, mark **Full view only**. In the "Content" field, click **Books**. Type our chosen keywords from page 50.

Now how many results are available?

_____

Better Ways to Use Google™ *(cont.)*

ONLINE

6. Now go back to the Advanced Search page and click on **Google News archive search**. This provides results from historical archives of news articles and primary resources. It can also generate time lines from applicable eras in history for added reference. Type "video games education."

    Now how many results are available?

    _____

7. Go to the Advanced Archive Search, and in the drop down menu for "Language," select **English** and for the date range, put in "2007" and "2009."

    Now how many results are available?

    _____

8. Last one! This time we're going to Google Blog Search, which displays blog posts that people have been written or produced on your topic. To go to Google Blog Search, type **http://blogsearch.google.com**. Type "video games in education."

    Now how many results are available?

    _____

9. Now click on **Advanced Blog Search**. Under the field marked "Dates," go to the drop-down menu that says **anytime** and set it to **last 12 hours.**

    Now how many results are available?

    _____

Better Ways to Use Google™ *(cont.)*

ONLINE

10. Go back to the Google homepage at **www.google.com**. Click on **Google Advanced Search**.

   Another little-used option is the drop-down list under "Need more tools?" that is marked "File Type." See the screen shot below that includes the choice you have after clicking on the drop-down menu:

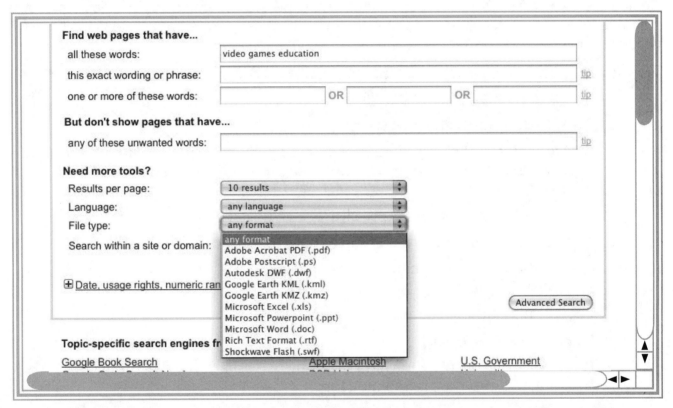

This searches by a specific file type. What this means is that if someone has made a Microsoft PowerPoint® presentation about your topic, you can narrow your search to just look for PowerPoint files. If you only want the information delivered in Flash Video format, you only have to ask.

Type "video games in education" in the "all these words:" field. Then go to "Need more tools" and drag the drop-down menu to search for **Microsoft PowerPoint (.ppt).**

Now how many results are available?

_____

As you can see, the more specific your search is, the more accurate your results are.

Being An Internet Detective: The Six Accuracy Steps Handout

The best part of the Internet is also the most suspicious part: the fact that anyone can write anything. The Internet is exciting because you have access to experts and information that your parents and grandparents never had access to. You can take a college level class, you can study any subject you want, and you can find the answers to almost anything. But it also means that anyone can put up a website that is false or misleading, and you don't want to fall for it.

Computers may be fast, but they aren't smart. That's where you come in. You need to check websites for accuracy before you use their information as fact. Here are six steps to check for accuracy:

☐ Use Your Common Sense

Ask questions. Asking questions is a sure sign of how smart you are. As you read website content, make sure you always ask yourself the following questions:

- Who is the author of this site?

- Is there evidence to support what the author is saying?

- Is there evidence somewhere that supports or disagrees with this author?

- Is this author biased?

☐ Verify the Evidence

Be a detective with everything you read. The answers all lie in the evidence. Keep on the lookout for:

- proper nouns

- dates

- important keywords

Take this embedded information to a search engine (like Google) and find other believable references to back up your information.

☐ Triangulate the Data

Look at the word "triangulate." The prefix is "tri-," which means _____. What this means is that if you can't find three sources to back up your fact, then you can't really know for sure if your fact is credible or not. Read suspiciously!

Being An Internet Detective:
The Six Accuracy Steps Handout *(cont.)*

☐ **Follow the Links**

To where a page links is as important as what information is on that actual page. Click on the external links to find the next layer of information about the author and his or her intent. Perhaps you'll be linked to an encyclopedia entry (reliable link), or perhaps you'll be directed to an Amazon or Café Press product (unreliable link). Don't fall for a website that's really an elaborate ad to sell someone's product or point of view!

☐ **Analyze The URL**

This is by no means foolproof, but it is a place to start in verifying the accuracy of the site.

☐ **Check the Publisher**

If possible, use websites like **easywhois.com** to check the background on the site to help you answer some of the questions in your head.

By checking off your accuracy checklist, you will have diminished the chances that you have fallen for a false website or a website that is more promotional than fact.

Congratulations! You are now an Internet Detective.

Offline

Use Your Common Sense

Determining the reliability of a website just boils down to using your common sense. Use your critical thinking skills, that "thinking cap" you may hear so much about, and decide for yourself if you are on a site that is worth using as a reference.

Let's look at a couple of examples:

Look at the screen shot from **http://www.zapatopi.net/treeoctopus**.

Use Your Common Sense *(cont.)*

Looks good, right? It's got some recognizable symbols like the ribbon-shaped tentacle to support the Endangered Tree Octopus. It has photos, for Pete's sake! Surely it must be real! But your head alarm should be going off for a number of reasons. Questions that should be flying around your brain might include:

- Why is the URL "zapatopi" when the site is about saving a supposedly endangered animal? Why isn't the name related to the site?

- Have you ever heard of a "tree octopus"? What do you know about an octopus that makes this ridiculous?

- Look at the pictures. Have you ever seen an octopus in a tree?

On the lines provided, make a bulleted list of elements on the site that, frankly, set off your "false website" alarm.

_____

_____

_____

_____

_____

_____

_____

_____

Use Your Common Sense *(cont.)*

Now let's look at a screen shot of **www.allaboutexplorers.com.** Using your common sense is also about reading the text. Sometimes the inaccuracies are embedded in facts and are hard to find.

The following passage is a Biography about Vasco da Gama. Using a highlighter or colored pen, underline the lines in the biography that just somehow don't seem right.

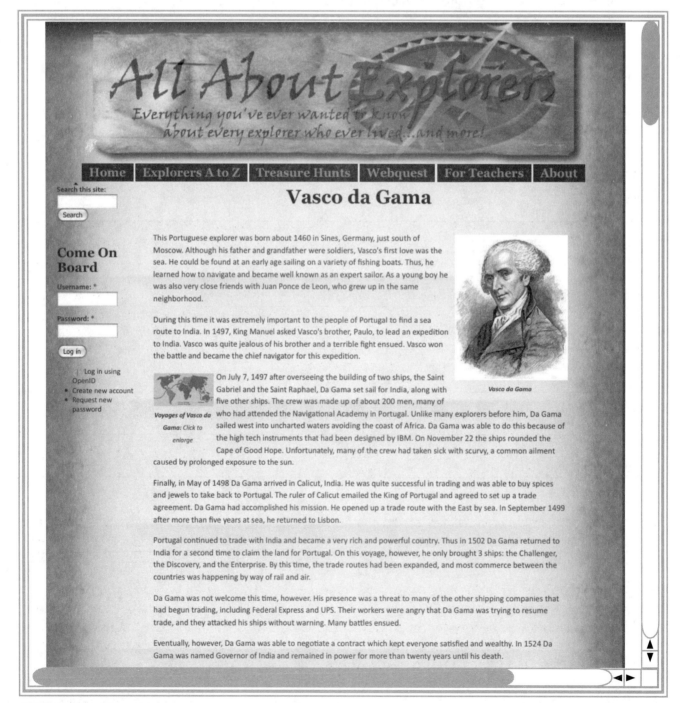

All About Explorers
Everything you've ever wanted to know about every explorer who ever lived...and more!

| Home | Explorers A to Z | Treasure Hunts | Webquest | For Teachers | About |

Search this site:
[Search]

Come On Board

Username: *

Password: *

[Log in]

Log in using OpenID
• Create new account
• Request new password

Vasco da Gama

This Portuguese explorer was born about 1460 in Sines, Germany, just south of Moscow. Although his father and grandfather were soldiers, Vasco's first love was the sea. He could be found at an early age sailing on a variety of fishing boats. Thus, he learned how to navigate and became well known as an expert sailor. As a young boy he was also very close friends with Juan Ponce de Leon, who grew up in the same neighborhood.

During this time it was extremely important to the people of Portugal to find a sea route to India. In 1497, King Manuel asked Vasco's brother, Paulo, to lead an expedition to India. Vasco was quite jealous of his brother and a terrible fight ensued. Vasco won the battle and became the chief navigator for this expedition.

Voyages of Vasco da Gama: Click to enlarge

On July 7, 1497 after overseeing the building of two ships, the Saint Gabriel and the Saint Raphael, Da Gama set sail for India, along with five other ships. The crew was made up of about 200 men, many of who had attended the Navigational Academy in Portugal. Unlike many explorers before him, Da Gama sailed west into uncharted waters avoiding the coast of Africa. Da Gama was able to do this because of the high tech instruments that had been designed by IBM. On November 22 the ships rounded the Cape of Good Hope. Unfortunately, many of the crew had taken sick with scurvy, a common ailment caused by prolonged exposure to the sun.

Finally, in May of 1498 Da Gama arrived in Calicut, India. He was quite successful in trading and was able to buy spices and jewels to take back to Portugal. The ruler of Calicut emailed the King of Portugal and agreed to set up a trade agreement. Da Gama had accomplished his mission. He opened up a trade route with the East by sea. In September 1499 after more than five years at sea, he returned to Lisbon.

Portugal continued to trade with India and became a very rich and powerful country. Thus in 1502 Da Gama returned to India for a second time to claim the land for Portugal. On this voyage, however, he only brought 3 ships: the Challenger, the Discovery, and the Enterprise. By this time, the trade routes had been expanded, and most commerce between the countries was happening by way of rail and air.

Da Gama was not welcome this time, however. His presence was a threat to many of the other shipping companies that had begun trading, including Federal Express and UPS. Their workers were angry that Da Gama was trying to resume trade, and they attacked his ships without warning. Many battles ensued.

Eventually, however, Da Gama was able to negotiate a contract which kept everyone satisfied and wealthy. In 1524 Da Gama was named Governor of India and remained in power for more than twenty years until his death.

Vasco da Gama

Verify the Evidence

You are writing an essay on a recently discovered indigenous tribe in Brazil. In order to write your paper, you have started your research by going to **www.wikipedia.com**. Now, because you are smarter than the computer, you know that just because the information is online, does not mean it's accurate. So you read the entry, keeping all the accuracy steps in mind.

The paragraphs below represent the possible Wikipedia entry. Keep in mind the following list of elements to look for when evaluating evidence:

- Proper Nouns

- Dates

- Important Keywords

In <u>May 2008</u>, The <u>Brazilian government</u> discovered one of South America's few remaining <u>uncontacted indigenous tribes</u>. In other words, this tribe has never before seen our modern civilizations or seen people outside of their tribal community.

Pictures taken by the Brazilian government depict red-painted tribe members with bows and arrows upraised, presumably pointing to the airplane flying overhead from which the picture was taken.

<u>Survival International's</u> director, <u>Stephen Corry</u>, says that the few remaining tribes such as these would "soon be made extinct" if outside groups don't work to protect their land. An official with <u>Brazilian government's Indian affairs department</u> is also quoted as saying that threats to these tribes and their land is "a monumental crime against the natural world" and "further testimony to the complete irrationality with which we, the 'civilized ones,' treat the world."

The pictures include <u>Malocas</u>, or communal structures with thatched roves. There appear to be two men with weapons drawn and a woman, all appearing to be in aggressive body paint like <u>urucum</u>, made from seeds of <u>the horse chestnut</u>. This dye is also used by other <u>Amazon tribes</u>.

Since we never just take Wikipedia's word as firm research, we know that we must follow up on what we've read with at least one more source. But which words or phrases are the most valuable to follow up on?

Each of the underlined words or phrases has been assigned a number value from one to three in the answer key on page 60. Circle the four most valuable words or phrases that you feel must be evaluated to verify the accuracy of the website. Only four have the maximum value of three, so if you want the most points, make sure you pick the words or phrases that you believe are the most important to verify with a follow-up search.

Verify the Evidence *(cont.)*

Answer Key

May 2008: 1 Point—Yes, this is important. But the date by itself is too general to be informative.

Brazilian Government: 1 Point—Again, while this is important, it is too general to be helpful in your search. If you were to just type this phrase into Google, you will have to go through a lot of results before you get to what you're looking for.

Uncontacted Indigenous tribes: 3 Points—Ah, this is a high-level phrase because it uses keywords that indicate exactly what you're trying to find.

Survival International: 3 Points— If you were to conduct a search on this organization, you would surely find the information you need. It's specific, and this group clearly knows about different tribes.

Stephen Corry: 3 Points—Looking up Stephen Corry may actually produce a search for ANY Stephen Corry. But it wouldn't take long, just a quick skim down the Google page, to find a link to the director of Survival International.

Brazilian government's Indian affairs department: 3 Points—great place to start. They would at least be able to point you in the right direction.

Malocas: 2 Points—this might just get you where you need to be, but a few links down the road. After all, other tribes may have used this kind of structure as well.

Urucum: 2 Points—Again, you'd learn about this particular dye, but it may not get you to the specific tribe you are looking for. At least it's the specific name of the dye, and not too general. It's just a little off-topic.

The Horse Chestnut: 1 Point —You might eventually find yourself at Urucum, but let's face it, there are easier ways to get to the information you need on the tribe.

Amazon tribes: 2 Points—while this is the topic, this as a phrase is not specific enough. Did you know that there are hundreds of Amazon tribes in the rain forest? You need to be more specific in your searching.

Analyze the URL

To know how to trust a site begins with being able to read. Yes, we know you can read, but can you translate what a URL breaks into?

Just as there are prefixes, roots, and suffixes in words, there are different parts to an online address. Some you may know already; some may be new to you.

1. Domain names are the root words of the URL. They come after the **http://www**. Domain names can give you hints about the purpose of the site as well as the reliability of the site. They might give you a hint as to whether a site is commercial or personal, both of which should be used for research with suspicion.

2. Extensions are abbreviated ways to show the organization that owns and publishes the website. Some common extensions are below.

Common Extensions

.edu = Educational organization (most US universities)

.k12 = many US school sites

.ac = academic institution (outside of US)

.sch = some schools outside US

.com = company (in UK it's usually .co)

.org = any organization

.gov = any government agency

.net= network

.mil = military institution

.biz, .name, .pro, .info = used for commercial purposes

Then there are also country codes like England's .uk or state codes like California's, which is .ca.

Keep in mind that even though some extensions are considered more reliable than others, none should be counted on for your sole source of research.

Remember that information from sites ending in .edu, .gov, and .k12 tend to be more reliable; while information from .com, .org, and .net sites always need more backup before you can use the research they provide.

Analyze the URL (cont.)

Here is an example of a URL in its entirety:

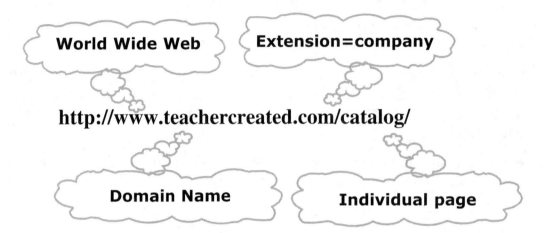

> **World Wide Web**
>
> **Extension=company**
>
> **http://www.teachercreated.com/catalog/**
>
> **Domain Name**
>
> **Individual page**

But sometimes you find yourself on a personal page, that is, a page created by an individual.

Critical Thinking Question: Why are personal pages unreliable?

_____

_____

_____

But there are clues that you can see in the URL, before you even click and read the page, before you even analyze the text, that should make you suspect a personal page.

Words like *Users* or *Members*, or symbols like ≈ or % give clues that it is a personal page and could be biased.

Deconstruct the following made-up URL, filling in the bubbles with your analysis.

http://www.teensrulz.biz/hdominic/.html

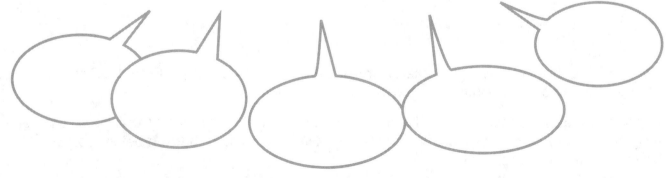

Check the Publisher

Finding the publisher of a website peels back layers that you won't see at first glance. For instance, **http://www.globalwarming.org** would seem like a great website if you were to be studying the effects of climate change, right? After all, it is a .org and it has your keyword as the domain name.

But if you go **to www.easywhois.com** you can peel back the first layer of research to reveal the true purpose of the website.

Go to **www.easywhois.com** and type in **www.globalwarming.org** and click **Next**.

You will see a huge list of information that was invisible to the person who just looked at the globalwarming.org webpage.

Answer the following questions to make sure you are reading the information accurately:

1. When was the website originally created?

    _____

2. What is the name of the registrant (the person who originally registered the domain name)?

    _____

3. What is the name of the Registrant Organization?

    _____

Uh-oh. If I were the researcher, I would definitely have my alarm going off in my head. A question in my head is: What does this organization have to do with global warming?

Let's find out.

Go to **www.google.com** and type in the registrant organization.

If you open up the website, you'll notice some things about the organization immediately that should lead you to believe that while this website gives information about global warming, it definitely has opinions about climate change that are **biased**. That is, the website is meant to persuade, not just inform.

Something to notice as well when being a good online detective is that there is a link in the corner that sends you right back to globalwarming.org.

This kind of circular research, where one website links to another that links back to the first, is not proof of reliability. In fact, it is very suspicious.

Also notice that there is a link directly below that connects to a shopping cart. In other words, this site is also meant to be an ad to promote products that support the organization's beliefs.

Online

Follow the Links

Now it's time to be a real website detective. Following the links is all about clicking off the page to determine the next layer of information and whether that information is really legitimate or not.

Let's go to **www.zapatopi.net/treeoctopus**. It's a great looking site, isn't it? It has photos, convincing information; it pleads for a convincing cause. But is it trustworthy?

But if we follow the links, we find that they dead-end at questionable places that certainly don't seem charitable!

Start clicking on the links that are provided. Write down the websites that they connect to. Perhaps they are a clue as to the legitimacy of the site.

Click on the icon in the most top-left hand corner of the page next to the letters ZPI. Where does it link?

_____

Hmmmm, "Productions," eh? Perhaps this is a produced site and not an informative one.

From the page you started on, click on the bumper sticker ad in the left-hand menu. Where does that connect you?

_____

But notice that there's a line on this page that says, "Learn more about this intelligent and inquisitive cephalopod at: zapatopi.net/treeoctopus/" What does that mean to you? That's right, it's circular research.

Circular research is when you click on one site, then follow a link that uses the first site as its primary link again. Think of it like a circle.

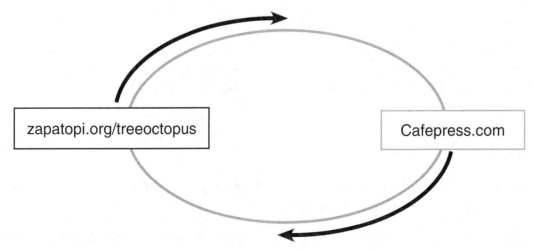

Evidence of legitimacy must come from external sites. A site can't prove all by itself that it is trustworthy. You have to explore beyond the site.

How to Cite Websites

Just as there is a proper format for citing books and magazines in a bibliography, there is a proper format for citing webpages. Citing acknowledges where you got the information. This is to not only give credit where credit is due, but to also give legitimacy to your own work.

To cite a webpage, you use the following formats:

A Website:

Author(s). <u>Name of page</u>. Date of Posting/Revision. Name of institution/organization affiliated with the site. Date of Access, URL.

Ex: Hylton, Jeremy. <u>The Complete Works of William Shakespeare</u>. Nov. 13, 2000. Massachusetts Institute of Technology. April 19, 2009. http://shakespeare.mit.edu/

An Article on a Website:

Author(s). "Article Title." <u>Name of page</u>. Date of Posting/Revision. Name of institution/ organization affiliated with the site. Date of Access, URL.

Ex: Dingman, Shane. "Stratford Shakespeare Festival puts 30 shows 'on hold'; recession blamed." <u>The Ampersand</u>. April 15, 2009. National Post. April 19, 2009. http://network. nationalpost.com/np/blogs/theampersand/archive/2009/04/15/stratford-shakespeare-festival-puts-30-shows-on-hold-recession-blamed.aspx

Remember, you always need to include the URL with your citation.

Bibliography Log

Let's say you must write an essay on the author J.R.R. Tolkien. Since you are expected to do research on a topic in a variety of ways, you must have research from at least two websites and one online article. Cite your websites and online article below.

(Much of the information can be found in the "About" page of a website or can be located at the very bottom of each site.)

Website:_____

URL: _____

Website:_____

URL: _____

Online Article: _____

URL: _____

Student-Friendly Websites Log

`ONLINE`

There are tons of different websites out there that can help a student research safely and efficiently. But at times they change and morph, disappear, or become outdated. It's important to have sites that you can go back to time and time again, but you should always keep your eyes open for new sites and resources to add to your box of research tools.

Below is a list of some great student-friendly research websites that have (so far) withstood the test of time. Check the links, however, before relying on them. In the meantime, however, we've provided lines so that you can also use this page as a log to add your own resources as you come across them.

The resources are broken down into genres to better serve you in your efficient search endeavors.

Search Engine Resources:
http://www.kidsclick.org
http://www.rcls.org/ksearch.htm
http://www.kids.yahoo.com
http://www.askforkids.com

_____

_____

News, Polls, Surveys:
http://www.timeforkids.com
http://www.scholasticnews.com
http://www.educationworld.com
http://www.edutopia.org

_____

_____

Science Info:
http://www.kidshealth.org
http://whyfiles.org

_____

_____

History Info:
http://rs6.loc.gov
http://timelines.com/

_____

_____

References:
http://www.encyclopedia.com
http://www.m-w.com
http://www.rhymezone.com
http://www.google.com

_____

_____

Biographies, Authors:
http://www.biography.com

_____

_____

ONLINE

Website Evaluation Form

Below is a website evaluation form. Use it to assess the trustworthiness and effectiveness of a website.

Name of the website you are evaluating:

_____

URL of website you are evaluating

http://_____

What does the URL extension translate to? (.com, .org, .gov., etc...)

_____

Are there any indications that this is a personal site? (#, *, ^, etc...)   Yes No

Please rate the following from 1–5, with 5 being most effective.

Do the graphics add to the page?

1	2	3	4	5

Is the author of the website clearly visible?

1	2	3	4	5

Can you easily find a link to a page about the author?

1	2	3	4	5

Is the spelling correct on the homepage?

1	2	3	4	5

Is there a banner that indicates the title/purpose of the site?

1	2	3	4	5

Are there effective headings and subheadings on the page that help chunk the information?

1	2	3	4	5

Is there a clear way to contact the author somewhere on the website?

1	2	3	4	5

ONLINE

Website Evaluation Form *(cont.)*

Is there an obvious date when the website was last updated? (generally found at the bottom of the homepage)

    1   2   3   4   5

Are the navigation (tabs, menu bars) of the page clear and easy to understand?

    1   2   3   4   5

On supporting pages, is there a link back to the home page that makes moving from page to page easy to do?

    1   2   3   4   5

Does the title give you a clue as to the website's purpose?

    1   2   3   4   5

Is that purpose or mission statement clearly defined on the homepage?

    1   2   3   4   5

Did the information/links lead you to other sources that were useful?

    1   2   3   4   5

Is the site biased? Does it clearly express an opinion?

    1   2   3   4   5

Is the page well-written (based on what you know about expository writing, persuasive, narratives, or literary analysis)?

    1   2   3   4   5

If the author is writing for a company or cause, is this affiliation clearly defined?

    1   2   3   4   5

Are the links that take you away from the site research based? Are they themselves seemingly reliable?

    1   2   3   4   5

Last Question: Is this a reliable website? Why or why not? _____

Basic Rules of Netiquette

"Netiquette" is the accepted word for online behavior. It refers to the expected manners that everyone should use when they are communicating on the Internet.

The following rules are important to remember when you are online:

1. **Treat others with courtesy and respect.** Don't be cruel. Just because you can't see a correspondent, doesn't mean he or she can't feel. Here's a good rule of thumb: if you won't say it to his or her face, then don't feel liberated to say it in writing. Also, bullying is bullying regardless of whether it is physically on the playground or written on a note, blog, or email. Remember that everything that is written online can be seen forever. Don't let your online footprint be one that shows evidence of cruelty.

2. **Don't use bad language.** Using bad language just proves you don't know how to say something well.

3. **Don't spread rumors or lies.** This is a form of bullying and is against the law (and can be enforced by the law, too). Use the Internet to spread information, not instigation. Words and writing are powerful. With the Internet, anyone has access to giving information and reading information. Treat that power with respect and don't abuse another person or your audience.

4. **DON'T SHOUT.** ALL CAPS = shouting. Use all caps sparingly, as you would a highlighter.

5. **Don't break the law.** Stealing from others isn't just impolite; it's illegal.

6. **Share your expertise.** The Internet allows people from all over the world to share their knowledge. It's hard to imagine a time when we couldn't just Google any answer. You also have an audience for what you can do well. There are people out there who want to know how to do something that you already know how to do. Share your knowledge.

Basic Rules of Netiquette *(cont.)*

7. **Lurk before you participate.** "Lurking" is a term for reading and exploring a site before writing a comment. Read thoroughly before participating in an online discussion or activity. Know your audience before they know you.

8. **Control flame wars.** "Flaming" happens when the fires of gossip get out of control and rapidly spread. Sometimes flame wars start because someone started a discussion without any thought of holding back his or her emotions, and had the intention to flame others. Sometimes a comment begins a flame war. Don't get caught up in it. Don't be the dry grass that helps the fire to burn out of control.

9. **Be forgiving.** Everyone's a newbie at sometime in his or her life. Everyone misspells occasionally or offends someone by accident because he or she hasn't perfected an email voice yet. Just remember that most people online are well intentioned and looking to communicate and learn. Let the small things pass, and pick your battles.

Basic Rules of Netiquette (*cont.*)

Look at the two scenarios below. Identify which rules of netiquette are being broken and list their numbers in the lines following each example.

Scenario #1

DBG#23: That guy in Mrs. J's class is awful! You should've heard what he said to me during class. It was like I was stupid or something. The teacher wanted a metaphor, right? Well, I've got one. That guy's as dumb as dirt! At least I have you to talk to.

COMMENT: Oh, he's not so bad.

DBG#23: Oh yeah? How would you know?

COMMENT: I AM that guy in Mrs. J's class.

Rules Broken: _____

Scenario #2

SGFD: HEY EVERYONE! I HOPE THAT YOU UNDERSTOOD MY ESSAY ON THE CELL. I HAD A GREAT TIME MAKING THE MODEL AND I EVEN HELPED MY SISTER UNDERSTAND IT BETTER TOO. SHE'S TWO YEARS YOUNGER, BUT NOW SHE'LL BE PREPARED.

PETERPIPER87: I thought your essay was really great. It included the cell membrane that I totally forgot to put into my model. Just so you know, you're yelling. No biggie. But all caps is hard to read. Thanks for the update!

Rules Broken: _____

Netiquette: Share Your Expertise

You are great at something. You are already an expert at something. What are you good at? What do you love to do?

In the space below, write a one-paragraph blog entry about something you are really great at or really love to do. Start by creating a headline or a catchy title for your entry. A good rule of thumb is that if you can teach it to someone younger than you, then you must be pretty good at it.

When you are finished writing, pass your paper to a classmate so that he or she can comment or inquire about your interest.

In your response post, remember to thank him or her for commenting!

_____

_____

_____

_____

_____

_____

_____

Comment: written by _____ on _____ at _____ pm

_____

_____

_____

Response

_____

_____

_____

_____

Extension Activity

Go online and see if there are other bloggers out there who share your passion. Remember, don't participate in a discussion thread until you've lurked around and you're sure the participants are appropriate for your age and interests.

Netiquette: How to Comment on a Blog

Online reading is meant to be very interactive. While there are those students who click around reading this and that, there are many who also comment on what they read. In fact, commenting is not only accepted, it's encouraged. Remember that just as there are classroom rules for responding to someone's writing and ideas, there are rules online when you are responding to a blog post or article. Here are some of the rules:

1. **Don't say anything you wouldn't say in person.** Just because you can't see the author doesn't mean he or she doesn't have feelings.

2. **Don't hijack the discussion.** Stay on topic.

3. **Bring something new to the conversation.**

4. **Don't be a know-it-all smarty-pants.** If you have to correct somebody, be polite. And you don't always need to be the one to correct somebody. Think of it like class: if all the students corrected each other every time someone misspoke or mispronounced, nobody would feel comfortable speaking out loud. It's the same online. It's more important to focus on the deeper content when reading.

5. **Make your tone clear.** Try not to use humor or sarcasm; they don't always go over well, even if you are the best writer ever. Use emoticons or write what the audience might see at that moment (shrug) to communicate your message clearer.

6. **Don't write anonymously.**

7. **Cite your sources with links.** If you mention a resource, link the words to the resource or provide the website for others to refer to.

8. **Paste quotes into your comment field.** If you are commenting on a quote within the post, copy and paste the quote into your comment field and then comment on it below so that the readers don't have to scroll back up to the original article.

9. **Don't comment when you are emotional.** If you are angry with someone for posting something, calm down before writing something that could forever be accessed. A good rule is to give it a day and then return to the post. Maybe even write a draft of your comment and let it lie for 24 hours. You can always cut and paste it into the comment field if you still believe it represents you well.

10. **Don't fan a flash fire.** A flash fire is when someone says something inflammatory and then people jump on the bandwagon, fanning the flames even more. If you ever see it happening, don't jump in. If there is a moderator, let him or her know what's happening. That will defuse it even faster.

Netiquette:
How to Comment on a Blog *(cont.)*

Activity

Below is an example of a blog entry about Persuasive Essay Writing. The author is a middle school student who has posted the article as an assignment for English class.

At the bottom of the post is a comment field. Fill it in with a paragraph that comments on the article. If you can refer to a website as a resource, that's even better.

Then, pass your paper to a peer, have him or her flip it over, and have him or her comment after you. He or she may either add a comment about the original article, or he or she may comment on something you said. Your peer must use formal paragraph form for his or her comment.

Then, the second student must pass the paper on to one more student to fill in his or her own comment, referring to either the original article or to one of the comments.

Persuasive Essay Writing

Posted by Annie Bain-Epling, 5/27/10, 8:06PM

I have always struggled with writing persuasive essays. I mean, I like to argue, but the format of a persuasive essay has always been a struggle. For instance, I don't understand the purpose of a counterargument. My word choice is also always weaker than I am feeling in my heart when I'm writing something I feel passionately about. Last year, I wrote an essay on the effects of global warming on polar bears, but it just came out, well, blah. I wish I had a toolbox of strategies to help me specifically with persuasive writing. I wouldn't mind a little advice if anyone's out there reading.

Post a Comment:

Ethics Online

Go to Google and type **Define: ethics.** According to Google, the definition of ethics is

_____.

This applies to our behavior online as well as in our everyday encounters with other people. The reason it's important to remind people of ethics online is because there is no one physically looking over your shoulder to remind you of how to behave while you are on the Internet. It's up to everyone to monitor him or herself.

There are basic ethical expectations that you need to learn so that you can function online in an appropriate and legal way. If you know right from wrong offline, then you should know right from wrong online.

Want to know your level of netiquette savvy?

Go to **http://www.learnthenet.com/english/flashtest/netiquette.htm** and take the quiz. (Remember to proofread your typing before hitting return. Typing a URL instead of cutting and pasting can lead to typos and then you never get where you need to go. So make sure you type the correct URL.)

Record your Score here _____.

Copyright 101

Copyrights are all around us. They are what protect a creator, writer, or inventor and his or her ideas. Sometimes your most precious possession is your intellectual property. That is, what you think of in your mind is yours if you register it with the federal copyright office before someone else does.

Every device you use was thought of and created by someone just like you: a pencil, a lightbulb, a TV, a computer, a scuba tank, and even that little plastic tip at the end of your shoelace was thought of by someone and registered with the copyright office.

Books have copyrights. Online articles may have copyrights. Songs have copyrights. Movies have copyrights. In other words, people thought of them, registered those thoughts as their own, and have the right to be paid whenever someone else wants to use them.

Ethics Online *(cont.)*

So let's say someone writes a song, and in fact, that's how she makes a living. She writes songs, gets payment if someone uses that song, and puts food on her table and a roof over her head. But with the onset of the Internet came ease in stealing people's intellectual property. Nowadays, it's almost commonplace to share songs with friends (Peer2Peer File Sharing) or rip movies from websites for free, sometimes even before they are available on CDs or DVDs. This is not legal. It's stealing.

Just as stealing a car from a neighbor's driveway is stealing, so is taking someone's intellectual property without paying for it.

So what falls under copyright law? Let's read what it says.

Go to **http://www.copyright.gov/fls/fl102.html.** Read the document and answer the following questions:

1. Fill in the blanks: It is the right of the owner of the copyright (the author, inventor, etc...) "to reproduce or to _____ others to reproduce the work in _____."

2. True or False (circle one): Reproduction is considered "fair use" when used in teaching.

3. True or False (circle one): A student may use a cited quote in school, but cannot use the piece of work in its entirety.

4. "The safest course is always to get _____ from the copyright owner before using copyrighted material."

So what happens if you get caught? To answer this question, let's look at one of the more controversial cases out there. Let's start by going to **www.wikipedia.com**.

In the search bar on the left, type in the name "Jammie Thomas." Jammie Thomas, as you will learn by reading the article, was fined almost two million dollars for her illegal filesharing habits.

Now, that's not to say that this is going to happen to any kid sharing songs, but it is what the law can allow to happen. Why? Because file sharing is illegal.

But the Recording Industry Association of America (RIAA) does have some resources available online for students looking to use free music. And there are other sites out there—some for free, and some for a small price—that provide access to their entire libraries. Here are just some that are out there:

www.riaa.com—for music download information (free)

www.soundzabound.com—royalty-free music library for education

www.pics4learning.com—free alternative to google images (which are copyrighted pictures)

www.istockphoto.com—inexpensive system allows users to purchase credits to be used towards a humongous database of photographs

Formal Writing Versus Texting

Look, we all know that there is a formal language that we use in the classroom when we communicate, whether it's through writing or talking. For instance, we don't use "isn't" in our formal writing; instead we use "is not." But we also know an online texting language has developed that requires its own literacy. The question is: does texting have a place in the classroom?

Many years ago, there was this written language of sorts called "shorthand." You could take classes in shorthand to learn how to write notes quickly. What if texting is the new shorthand? Perhaps it can be used for note taking and brainstorming.

Learning how to write in the language of texting has a place in the classroom when you have to take notes quickly. When you are studying later, you will need to be able to translate what you wrote. It is also very valuable to then look at your notes and write them out in formal language as a way to help memorize the material.

Translation activities

1. Look at the excerpt from the texting dictionary below. Use it as a guide in translating the lines below which are written in texting.

lol = laugh out loud	idk = I don't know
ttul = talk to you later	omg = oh my gosh
u = you	jk = just kidding
c = see	2 = to/too
ne = any	2mrw = tomorrow
b4 = before	b/c = because

OMG, I just got my grade back 2day in history. I got a C b/c I couldn't find my textbook. Jk, I got a B. Idk when the homework's due, do u?

_____

_____

2. Something interesting about texting is that it is a language that is constantly evolving and new "words" are invented every day, even by students like you. What new texting words can you invent and add to your dictionary? Can you think of ways to shorthand words from your history class? From your math class? Write three subject-specific words on the lines below and then translate them into the texting words on the opposite lines provided.

_____   _____

_____   _____

_____   _____

Formal Writing Versus Texting *(cont.)*

3. How well do you know standard text-message language? Draw a line from the text message on the left to its "translation" in formal English on the right.

1) c u l8r m8	a) as far as I know
2) b4	b) love you with all my heart
3) afaik	c) boring
4) w8 4 me, i'm l8, soz	d) text me back
5) kit	e) Have a nice day.
6) ruok?	f) See you later, mate.
7) luwamh	g) keep in touch
8) hand	h) easy
9) zzzzzzzzz	i) Are you okay?
10) tmb	j) Wait for me, I'm late, sorry.
11) 0 me	k) See you tonight or tomorrow.
12) ez	l) by the way
13) btw	m) before
14) c u 2nite O 2mrw	n) Ring me.

4. Is it always appropriate to use texting? Probably not. In the boxes below, judge when it is acceptable to use texting. Discuss each of them with your class after you have made your prediction.

Texting Contexts	Good idea?	Bad idea?
You want to ask somebody out on a first date.		
You want to wish a friend happy birthday.		
You want to say sorry to a friend for a mistake you made.		
You need to ask for a website as a resource from someone who may know.		
Your school wants to keep in touch with parents.		
You need to tell a parent or guardian where you are located.		

5. In the lines below, write your own paragraph writing in texting language. Your teacher will give you a subject from class to use as your topic.

_____

_____

Now, switch texting essays with a peer and write his or her texting paragraph into a formal essay language.

The Importance of Teaching Social Site Literacy in Schools

Kids go on social websites by the droves. They are reading and interacting with no formal lessons in how to do so. And schools thus far have not played a part in helping teach students how to interact. It's happening and we need to be a part of it.

Social websites range from places like Facebook, which initially started as a music group networking site, to YouTube. Facebook allows people to find other people with commonalities, follow them through their day, and share pictures in online albums. You may belong to an alumni group, or find people who all like gardening. You might only share your page with family members, or you might invite people who share your same passion for playing soccer. YouTube is a place to post videos of any subject. You can create your own network with its own themes, get recommendations from others, or subscribe to someone's video feed.

Both Facebook and YouTube represent a growing trend in online interaction. It's undeniable. But the vast ocean of information and accessibility can also be scary. For those reasons, we need to teach students how to read pages from social websites like these so that they can make wise decisions rather than stumble on impropriety.

The worksheets on the following pages explore how to read a TeacherTube homepage as well as how to interact with Twitter. While these pages are intended for student learning, it is possible that you, the teacher, may learn from them as well. It is sometimes only our trepidation that keeps us from exploring the educational benefits of new technology.

Perhaps this section might help demystify some of what holds us back from teaching the literacies that this generation of students need.

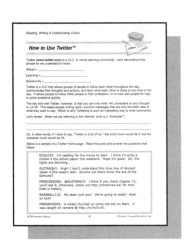

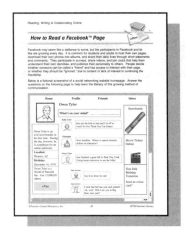

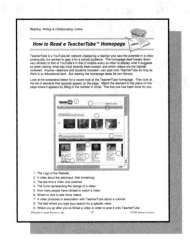

What Is a Blog?

Materials

Index cards, pens or pencils, sticky notes

Directions

1. Distribute an index card to each student and on it, have him or her write about his or her favorite book, mentioning the author, title, genre, and a brief summary.

2. Post these cards up around the room and distribute sticky notes to the class.

3. Have the students conduct a gallery walk around the classroom, leaving comments on sticky notes underneath the cards that they want to comment on.

4. Let students know that there can be no more than three comments for each card and that they must comment on at least five cards. Also, have them place their sticky notes in a vertical chain, one after the other (rather than just slap them on the card), to show the order of the comments.

5. When everyone is done, have them return to the cards they commented on and have them comment one more time. This time, they may comment again about the main topic, or comment about someone else's comment.

Congratulations! Your students have just created offline blogs.

Blogs are journal entries that are interactive. That is, people can comment on an entry and the author can comment back. So, unlike a diary, it's transparent. Blogs are used to share information about specific topics. Some people have blogs about their life, some on their hobbies, some on how to do their job. Whatever the topic, a blog is a great way to experiment with writing about a particular issue or theme, and seeing if anyone else out there is interested in it, too.

For an online explanation of what a blog is, go to **http://www.commoncraft.com/blogs.**

There are many quick, free, and easy ways to set up blogs: **www.blogger.com** and **www. thinkquest.com** to name two.

Extension Activity

Just like in the above video by CommonCraft, have students design their own pictorial explanation of a blog.

What Is a Wiki?

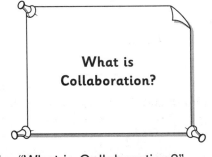

Materials

Posters, Markers

Directions

1. Divide your students into small, working groups.

2. Give a large, poster-sized paper to each group.

3. At the top of the poster, have one person write the topic, "What is Collaboration?"

4. Rotate the poster so that each person in the group comments in the topic, signing his or her name at the end of the last comment.

5. Send the poster rotating once more around the same group and have people delete repetitive words, select better word choices, and correct any errors they may see.

6. Have them consider each person's contributions as they combine the brainstorming notes to a single sentence that answers the topic question.

Congratulations! Your students have just created an offline wiki.

Wikis are a tool used in collaboration. They provide a forum where people can brainstorm together, edit and revise, and publish their efforts. They can be on any subject, include any number of people, and be available to contribute to for any finite or indefinite length of time. They are excellent for small group collaboration.

For a short online explanation of wikis, go to
http://www.commoncraft.com/video-wikis-plain-english.

There are many companies out there who provide free and easy online ways to create wikis—
www.PBWiki.com and **www.Google.com** to name just two.

Extension Activity

Just like in the above video by CommonCraft, have students design their own pictorial explanation of what a wiki is.

How to Use Twitter™

Twitter (**www.twitter.com**) is a VLC, or virtual learning community. Let's deconstruct that phrase so we understand it more.

Virtual = _____

Learning = _____

Community = _____

Twitter is a VLC that allows groups of people to follow each other throughout the day, communicate their thoughts and actions, and learn what each other is doing at any time of the day. It allows people to follow other people in their profession, or to even ask people for help to solve questions quickly.

The key trick with Twitter, however, is that you can only write 140 characters or your thought is cut off. This keeps people writing quick, succinct messages that are only the main idea of what they want to say. Which is why Twittering is such an interesting way to write summaries.

Let's review: When we are referring to the Internet, what is a "character"?

_____

_____

So, in other words, if I were to say, "Twitter is a lot of fun," the word count would be 6, but the character count would be 23.

Below is a sample of a Twitter Home page. Read the posts and answer the questions that follow.

KOOLCAT: I'm waiting for the movie to start. I think I'll write a review 4 the school paper this weekend. Hope it's good. Oh, the lights are dimming...

GUITARGUY: Argh! I don't understand this time line of Ancient Japan 4 this week's test! Anyone out there know the era of the Samurai?

PRINCESSDEE: @GUITARGUY: I think if you check chapter 12, you'll see it, otherwise, check out http://timelines.ws/ for time lines in history.

BASEBALL132: My team just won! We're going to state! Wish us luck!

MARSROVERS: A wheel churned up some red soil on Mars. It was caught on camera @ http://tr.im/i1vG.

How to Use Twitter™ *(cont.)*

1. Who needs help studying for his or her history exam?

   _____

2. What website does PRINCESSDEE recommend that a person search to answer the question about Ancient Japan?

   _____

3. What person do you follow to get the latest updates from Mars?

   _____

4. What is the symbol used that indicates that a person is "tweeting" directly to another person?

   _____

Below, we're going to track our thoughts as we would on Twitter.

1. First, decide on a screen name. Make it 5–10 letters and/or numbers in length.

   _____

2. Create a post that is 120–140 characters in length that tells your classmates about what is on your mind right at this instant.

   _____

   _____

   _____

Extension Activity

Create a chart in the classroom that allows each student to add his or her post in a list. This "Twitter Chart" is a snapshot of the thoughts of the class written in 140 characters or less.

Metacognitive Crossover

Create a notebook page for "Tweets" in students' writing notebooks or binders. On occasion, stop your lesson and ask your students to add to the "Twitter page," capturing their thoughts at that moment. Create a chart that displays the questions or comments that students may have as written in "Twitter" format.

Twitter™ *as Literary Response*

Twitter (**www.twitter.com**) is a VLC, or virtual learning community. That is, it allows a group of people to follow each other throughout the day and communicate their thoughts and actions.

Twitter allows people to follow other people in their profession, or to even ask people for help to solve questions quickly.

The key trick with Twitter, however, is that you can only write 140 characters or your thought is cut off. This keeps people writing quick, succinct messages that are only the main idea of what they want to say. Which is why Twittering is such an interesting way to write summaries.

Let's review: When we are referring to the Internet, what is a character?

_____

_____

So, in other words, if I were to say, "I would rather read the book than see the movie," the word count would be 10, but the character count would be 47.

Think about a story that you have read this year. Write a Twitter update (or "tweet") a summary that is only 120–140 characters in length here:

_____

_____

_____

Now think about that story's theme. Tweet the theme of the story using only 120–140 characters in length here:

_____

_____

_____

How does the main character change in the story? Tweet your response on the lines provided: _____

_____

_____

What is the turning point of the story? _____

_____

_____

Any question can be answered as a tweet as a means to collaborate or brainstorm prior to a more formal essay. Try it next time.

How to Read a Facebook™ Page

Facebook may seem like a dalliance to some, but the participants in Facebook and its like are growing every day. It is common for students and adults to host their own pages, download their own photos into albums, and share their daily lives through short statements and comments. They participate in surveys, share videos, and join clubs that help them understand their own identities, and publicize their personality to others. People decide whether someone can be called a "friend" and has access to interact with their page, or whether they should be "ignored," due to content or lack of interest in continuing the friendship.

Below is a fictional screenshot of a social networking website homepage. Answer the questions on the following page to help learn the literacy of this growing method of communication.

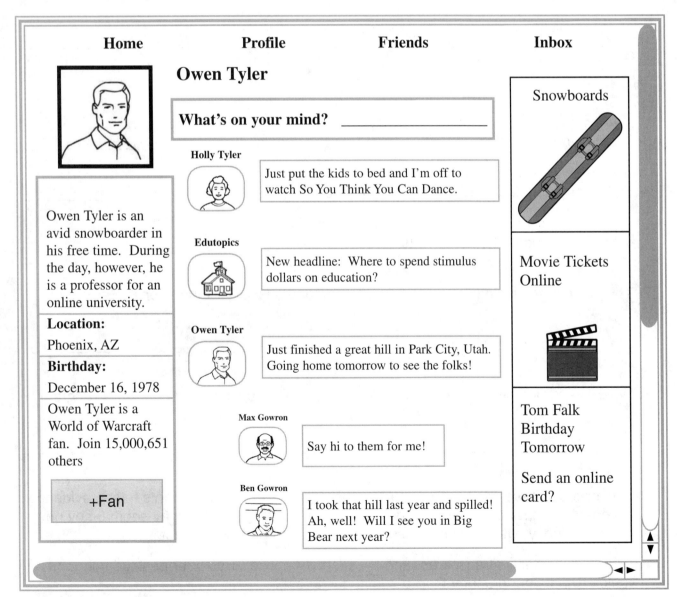

Home	Profile	Friends	Inbox

Owen Tyler

What's on your mind? _____

Owen Tyler is an avid snowboarder in his free time. During the day, however, he is a professor for an online university.

Location:
Phoenix, AZ

Birthday:
December 16, 1978

Owen Tyler is a World of Warcraft fan. Join 15,000,651 others

+Fan

Holly Tyler
Just put the kids to bed and I'm off to watch So You Think You Can Dance.

Edutopics
New headline: Where to spend stimulus dollars on education?

Owen Tyler
Just finished a great hill in Park City, Utah. Going home tomorrow to see the folks!

Max Gowron
Say hi to them for me!

Ben Gowron
I took that hill last year and spilled! Ah, well! Will I see you in Big Bear next year?

Snowboards

Movie Tickets Online

Tom Falk Birthday Tomorrow

Send an online card?

How to Read a Facebook™ Page *(cont.)*

1. Who is the owner of this homepage? _____

2. What is his profession? _____

3. In what section do you enter your own thoughts, updates, or comments? _____

4. How many people are in the World of Warcraft club? _____

5. Which two people commented on Owen's last entry? _____

   _____

   _____

6. What is the sponsored ad on this page trying to sell you? _____

7. How many personal entries are on this first page? _____

8. What is the age of the person whose page this is? _____

9. This page is reminding its owner to wish someone a Happy Birthday on the next day.

   Who needs birthday wishes? _____

10. Where can I find other people you know who are also registered users of this program?

    _____

Recently, colleges have been trolling the Facebook pages of their applicants to see evidence of questionable behavior. In other words, pictures and comments that may seem funny now may not be so funny later. It's not an issue of privacy; it's an issue of tact.

The point is, everything's transparent and lives forever online. Use your best judgment. If you wouldn't want your grandmother to see it, don't post it.

How to Read a TeacherTube™ Homepage

Offline

TeacherTube is a YouTube-ish network created by a teacher who saw the potential in a video posting site, but wanted to gear it for a school audience. The homepage itself breaks down very similarly to that of YouTube's in that it morphs every so often to display what it suggests as great viewing, what has most recently been posted, and which videos are the highest reviewed. Anyone—teachers and students included—can post onto TeacherTube as long as there is an educational bent. But reading the homepage takes its own literacy.

Look at the screenshot below for a recent look at the TeacherTube homepage. Then look at the list of elements that typically appear on the page. Match the element to the place on the page where it appears by filling in the number in circle. The first one has been done for you.

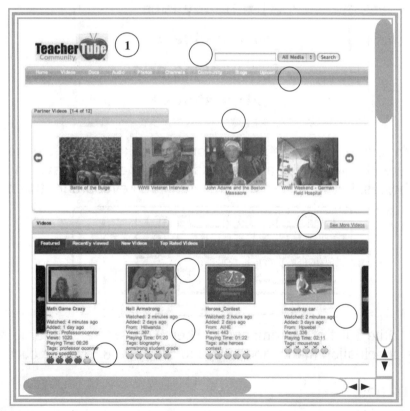

1. The Logo of the Website
2. A video about the astronaut, Neil Armstrong
3. The last time a video was watched
4. The icons representing the ratings of a video
5. How many people have clicked to watch a video
6. Where to click to see more videos
7. A video produced in association with TeacherTube about a colonist
8. The field where you type your search for a specific video
9. Where you go after you've filmed a video in order to post it onto TeacherTube

Emoticons: Adding Emotions to Short Texts

This activity is a fun way to help you learn where the punctuation is on a keyboard. Emoticons are another way to send text messages. They are nonlinguistic methods of communication through little pictures made out of punctuation marks. They also serve another purpose. In the online world, we don't get the chance to see people's faces and expressions. Sometimes our words need expressions in order for the audience to truly understand our meaning. Emoticons help the writer to expand their intentions for the reader. Here are some examples:

> **:-) = happy face**
>
> **:-(= sad face**
>
> **;-D = winking grin**
>
> **xD = shock**

First things first, let's review where the punctuation is on a keyboard. On the keyboard below, color the keys that are obvious punctuation marks. Now, there are ways on the computer to insert even more choices, but we'll start with the standard keyboard for this basic activity.

On the lines below, write a list of five emotions. Then work with a partner to see if you can use the keyboard's punctuation marks and letters to create your own emoticons.

Frustration
_____   _____

_____   _____

_____   _____

_____   _____

_____   _____

Dynamic Versus Static Documents

Go to **www.google.com.** In the search bar, type "define: static." Write the first definition that appears on the lines below:

_____ _____

_____ _____

Now type "define: dynamic." On the lines below, write the first definition that appears.

_____ _____

_____ _____

These two words have been used to describe the status of documents. That is, a static document is one that may be your traditional multi-paragraph essay. Perhaps it has a bibliography at the end and the occasional footnote at the bottom of each page.

But essays have evolved. These traditional essays are static or, in other words, flat. That is, they are only as layered as the black and white ink on their surface.

But a dynamic, or full, document is one that is full of texture.

Two ways to create a textured, dynamic document are:

- adding graphics
- providing links

Where to Go for Free Images to Add Graphics to Your Document

It isn't just adding links that makes your document dynamic. Adding graphics is also an important part of adding texture, research, and uniqueness to your essays.

You can use the following websites for free, education-friendly images:

http://www.pics4learning.com/

http://memory.loc.gov/ammem/index.html

Be careful! Many students are tempted to just go to Google Image Search™ in order to swipe some pictures to add texture to their document. But remember, this is illegal, and the images on Google are not screened for appropriateness. Major rules of netiquette are breached by copying and pasting images from Google, so don't do it!

Dynamic Versus Static Documents *(cont.)*

How to Add Links to Your Document

Just as accurate and varied links are a good sign of the legitimacy of a wikipedia entry, so are links a good sign of valuable research in a student's essay. Now, mind you, it isn't a sure sign of validity, but it's important to get in the habit of creating dynamic documents that give your reader additional locations in which they can continue their own research.

Let's practice creating links on a document.

1. Type the following phrase:

"Sir James M. Barrie was the author of *Peter Pan*."

(*Note:* You'll notice that the title of the book is in italics rather than underlined. That's because when you link text to a webpage, it is automatically underlined to indicate to the reader that it's actually a link. More and more formal documents are using italics to highlight book titles for this reason.)

2. Now highlight the name of the author, James M. Barrie.

Go to Insert in the Menu Bar and click Hyperlink. Type the following website URL:

http://www.jmbarrie.co.uk/

This is the website for J. M. Barrie's biographer, who wrote *J. M. Barrie and the Lost Boys*.

3. Now highlight the word "Sir." Go to Insert > Hyperlink and type in the following website URL:

http://www.royal.gov.uk/MonarchUK/Honours/Knighthoods.aspx

This is the official website for the British Monarchy and includes all sorts of facts about their history and current functions.

4. Now highlight the words, "*Peter Pan*." Open up your browser and go to **www.amazon.com**. Find the book *Peter Pan*. After you find it, copy the URL for that Amazon book page and paste it into the Hyperlink box so that when a reader clicks on the words in your document, he or she will be connected to the Amazon page.

Clearly, linking text can go on forever. Make sure you only use the power of linking as a means to give more important information to your reader. Have you ever seen a page of notes that's been over-highlighted? Well, avoid that scenario by making sure that you link purposefully. Don't over-link.

Offline Extension Activity: Now, if you don't have access to a computer, you can still practice this important skill.

1. Write a paragraph about something you are currently learning in your history class. It should be at least 5–10 sentences in length.

2. Underline any proper nouns, dates, or important common nouns. These underlined words represent terms that you might link to webpages in a more formal document.

ONLINE

Book Reviews

There are great websites on which to write book reviews. Many public libraries, school sites, and educational websites have pages of student-created book reviews. These reviews are read by an audience of thousands or even millions of people. Nowadays, people online are seeking opinions from other real people like you. Your review helps others to find their next well-loved books.

Review the format that Amazon.com uses and write a rough draft of a book review. It will only be one paragraph in length, so make sure that everything you write is important enough to be read. Prioritize what you believe is important enough to share in your writing.

Step 1: Pick a book that you read and really liked this school year.

Step 2: Include the T.A.G. in your main topic sentence (title, author, genre).

Step 3: Write a two-to-three sentence summary of the book.

Step 4: Write three characteristics that you like about the book. Think about what you know about Narratives. You've learned about plot, character traits, figurative language, conflict, etc...so select what you liked and focus on the top three reasons you liked the book.

Step 5: End with a persuasive line, using convincing word choice, about buying and reading the book.

On the lines below, write your rough draft paragraph combining all five steps. Remember to use transitional words and phrases to smooth out your sentence fluency.

_____

_____

_____

_____

_____

_____

_____

_____

_____

_____

_____

Design Your Own Website

Using what you now know about how to read a website and what goes into creating eye-catching, informative content, you are now going to design a website that represents you. (If it helps, look back at your prior worksheets. You can use these to help you make decisions as you design your own page.)

At the top, create a **banner**. It should include a **symbol** that represents who you are or what your interests are. It should also include your **theme**, a line that works like your very own **slogan** to tell people who come to your website what the **tone** of your site is.

There should be a **menu bar** with the following **tabs**:

Home, Blog, About, Book Reviews

The rest of the homepage is for you to decide. Now that you have read and analyzed webpages, what do you think works? Sketch your personal website in the box provided. You can use any medium you wish: pens, pencils, etc.—just remember it should represent you.

Student-Created Post Assessment

Are you feeling more Internet savvy now? After all, you've studied everything from the rules of netiquette to reliable research techniques. You've learned about TeacherTube and Twitter. You've rated websites and designed your own.

Look back on our original Internet Savvy Assessment. You rated your knowledge of how to function online. Now, rescore your knowledge of the same topics. Do you know more about these topics than you did at the beginning of these lessons?

Topic	4 (I could teach this subject, that's how much I understand it.)	3 (I get it, and I understand its purpose.)	2 (I get the gist of these things, but I still need a brush up on occasion.)	1 (What the heck is this?)
Netiquette				
Advanced Google Searches				
Twitter				
Identifying False Websites				
Evaluating a Good Website				
Online Collaboration				
Reading a Webpage				

Student-Created Post Assessment

Now you get to design your own assessment that reflects some of the lessons you've learned. Fill in the rubric below with the topics that you believe are the most important when going online successfully, safely, and efficiently.

Topic	4	3	2	1

Exchange your rubric with another student and fill it out. How much does he or she know now?

Answer Key

Page 12—Internet Savvy Pre-Assessment
Answers will vary from student to student.

Page 13—Internet Terminology
Answers will vary depending on website.

Page 15—What Constitutes a Reading Genre?
Answers will vary depending on discussion.

Page 17-18—Acceptable Use Policy Literary Analysis
1. F
2. F
3. D
4. Answers will vary.
5. Answers will vary.
6. Answers will vary.
7. www.cybercrime.gov
8. Answers will vary.
9. Answers will vary.

Page 22—Internet Literacy Vocabulary Crossword

Page 28—Identifying the Parts of a Website
1. Edutopia – What works in public education
2. Smart Interactive Boards
3. "Fostering Student Feedback," "What Parents Think About Student Achievement," "Spring Cleaning Your Classroom"
4. Jalen
5. 2009 Webby Award for the Best Education Site

Page 34—What Are Your Eyes Doing?
1. About, Blog, Resources, Contact
2. 3
3. 1
4. 5
5. 4
6. 2

Page 38—What's the Purpose of the Website?
1. teachers
2. Answers vary
3. School Issues
4. Apple, Schoolhouse, Answers will vary.
5. Deals of the Day

Page 48—How To Read a Google Search Page
1. Answrs will vary.
2. Answers will vary.
3. Answers will vary.
4. www.epa.gov/globalwarming/kids
5. 3
6.–9. Answers will vary (see bottom of the Google page).
10. 36, 800,000

Page 71—Basic Rules of Netiquette
1. 1, 3, 8
2. 4

Page 83—How to Use Twitter
1. Guitarguy
2. http://timelines.ws
3. Marsrovers
4. @

Page 86—How to Read a Facebook Page
1. Owen Tyler
2. professor for an online university
3. profile
4. 15, 000, 651
5. Max Gawron and Ben Gawron
6. Snowboards or Movie Tickets
7. 5
8. Answers will vary—look to birthday for correct response
9. Tom Falk
10. Friends

Page 93—Student-Created Post Assessment
Answers will vary.

Technology Resources

Websites

21st Century Information Fluency
http://21cif.com/
Alan November
http://novemberlearning.com/
BBC's Webwise
http://www.bbc.co.uk/webwise
British Council's Texting for All
http://www.teachingenglish.org.uk
Cybersmart!
http://cybersmartcurriculum.org
Dept. of Justice: Computer Crime and Intellectual Property
www.cybercrime.gov
iSafe
http://www.isafe.org/
Kathy Schrock's Guide for Educators
http://school.discovery.com/schrockguide/evalhigh.html
Netiquette by Virginia Shea (online edition)
http://www.albion.com/netiquette/book

Online Dictionaries

www.networkdictionary.com
en.wiktionary.org
en.wikipedia.org
infosat.tamu.edu
wordnetweb.princeton.edu
www.learn-english-today.com/vocabulary/computer_vocab.htm

Books

Using Google and Google Tools in the Classroom, Teacher Created Resources

Blogging in the Classroom, Teacher Created Resources

Media Literacy, Teacher Created Resources